Michael, JOE,
    PROUD Leaders, PROUD Family
Good Luck in the Business.

Rocky

TIGHTEN
THE LUG NUTS

THE PRINCIPLES OF
BALANCED LEADERSHIP

ROCKY **ROMANELLA**

3SIXTY MEDIA
C/O 3SIXTY Management Services, LLC
www.3sixtymanagementservices.com

ISBN: 978-0-9983863-0-0

"A heartfelt book that details the secret sauce required to craft an effective leadership strategy for today's challenging business world. *Tighten the Lug Nuts* will delight and disturb you in the best way. The elements of balanced leadership come alive through the poignant story of one manager's career journey from entry level through senior management."

—RICHARD SNOWDEN,
Senior Partner at RavenHouse International and
Author of *The Complete Guide to Buying a Business*

"Rocky Romanella has written a highly useful and highly readable book for ANYONE wishing to be a more effective (and happy) leader. His story-telling approach makes the book an entertaining read, and the lesson summaries that complete each chapter serve as a blueprint for putting the information into practice. I'd recommend *Tighten the Lug Nuts* to new leaders as well as experienced leaders. If you don't learn something from this book, you're not trying!"

—DENNIS SNOW,
Speaker, Consultant, and Author of *Unleashing Excellence: the Complete Guide to Ultimate Customer Service* and *Lessons from the Mouse*

"Rocky is an expert at leadership instruction through story-telling and has created a guide that any manager can relate to and put immediately into practice. Joe Scafone's experiences are parables written by an author who practiced what he preached. These lessons are authentic and timeless!"

—W. TIM DAVIS,
President at The UPS Store, Inc.

"We can only be successful and balanced leaders when we recognize our own ability to influence and empower others by listening, coaching, knowing what we stand for and what we can never compromise. Joe Scafone personifies how wisdom, confidence and humor derived from interactions with family, friends, colleagues and strangers over a lifetime can help train all of us to be the great listeners and leaders of our time. *Tighten the Lug Nuts: The Principles of Balanced Leadership* is a resource for all aspiring and current leaders."

—KAREN A. PASSARO,
Dean, Continuing Education and Professional
Studies at Seton Hall University

DEDICATION

To my beautiful wife Debbie.
She is the embodiment of 1 Corinthians 13:4-12. She is Love.

Love is patient, love is kind. It does not envy, it does not boast, it is not proud. It does not dishonor others, it is not self-seeking, it is not easily angered, it keeps no record of wrongs. Love does not delight in evil but rejoices with the truth. It always protects, always trusts, always hopes, always perseveres. Love never fails.

Thank You, Hon.

SPECIAL THANKS

To my family, Mom, Aunt Katie, and siblings, who were always supportive and integral parts of a childhood filled with love and lasting memories. To my dad, who instilled in all his children the values of hard work, integrity, and respect.

To my wonderful Children, Jean Marie, Nicole, Rocky, and Andrew. I cannot be prouder as a dad, more blessed as a father and grateful for all of your support throughout this journey.

To my friends and business partners too numerous to name. I thank you and Joe Scafone thanks you.

PREFACE

This book began as a tribute to a wonderful family and in grateful respect for an excellent career that I feel very fortunate and blessed to have lived, learned from, and experienced. It also gave me an opportunity to recognize and say thank you to two very influential people in my life, my dad, Pasquale, and my thoughtful, caring wife, friend, and partner, Debbie Romanella. Affectionately known as "the Hon."

I would like to add a third, you the reader. I realize that we all have very busy lives and time is that precious commodity that once spent we can never get back. I thank you for spending your time with me and my family. I hope you find my humble attempt to write a fun, thoughtful, and inspirational leadership book time well spent.

Leadership is something we all have concerns about. Leadership is a concept that is not reserved for or only applies to certain people in business, government, and civic organizations. The reality is that no matter our age, gender, occupation, educational level, or position in life, each of us touches and influences other lives.

Through this extension we are all leaders to someone at some time. It can be a person under our supervision or care, a spouse we honor and live with, or a child we nurture, a student we teach, or a player we coach. It could be as simple as a fellow member of our church or religious affiliation, club, league or association, but it is usually identified by the fact we have made a positive difference through our actions and examples.

With this sense of responsibility and being lifelong learners, we are constantly in pursuit of knowledge, whether written or experienced, of how to be a good leader and how to improve our skills. We take great pride in the books we have read and where they sit on the best-seller list.

I often find that some of the best examples and learning experiences come from the stories we tell and the experiences we share. Sometimes they come from the stories we learned as children or read to our children as parents or grandparents.

Leaders must develop emotional intelligence along with their educational intelligence and business acumen. Sometimes a simple story I find can help people see the bigger picture, promote moral and ethical behavior, and maybe, just maybe, not take ourselves so seriously that we lose sight of the fact that it is not always about us.

So here is the story I have chosen to start the book. I hope you enjoy this, and the many stories you will read throughout.

A wonderful person and woman well into her nineties is approaching the end of her life. Realizing the end is near, she scheduled a meeting with the pastor at her local church who she has chosen to coordinate her funeral. At the end of the meeting she looks at the pastor and tells him that she has one final but important request.

Anticipating what he thinks will be her final request, he tells her not to worry: he will give her last rites and absolution. He continues, "I am sure you will be forgiven for all your sins and should have a speed pass into heaven."

With a chuckle she thanks him but goes on to say, "That is not my request. My request is to be waked and buried with a fork in my hand." With a puzzled look he assures her he will execute her request. "Can I be so bold as to ask why?"

She proceeds to tell him, that when she was a child growing up, family meals were very important and always a highlight. Dinner was family time. After the main course, as the table was being cleaned, her mom would tell all the children to hold onto their forks, as the best was yet to come: dessert!

It always gave them something to look forward to. "As people pay their respects and they ask you why there is a fork in my hand," she explained, "I would like you to assure them that I left peaceful and happy, and I would like them to always look forward with the knowledge and view that the best is yet to come."

As you read through the many stories and lessons, I hope you enjoy the meal and as you finish the book, you still have your fork in your hand with the anticipation that the best for you is yet to come.

With great respect and thanks.

INTRODUCTION

I believe the definition of a successful leader can be summarized as a person who adds immediate value as a trusted advisor, mentor, and visionary who uses a process approach to lead the organization and its people to new levels of success. Great organizations need to have a thoughtful vision and strategy. Great leaders need to combine that strategic vision with the ability to tactically execute the strategy.

Leadership is about building a bridge to the future. You give your people the opportunity to help build that bridge by communicating and educating each one of them on your vision and strategy.

Leadership is the ability to quickly, accurately, and effectively assess

- who you are,
- what you stand for, and
- what you will never compromise.

It is important to take inventory and to be constructively dissatisfied in yourself to make sure that your vision and strategy correspond to what your people, your customers, and investors believe to be your strategy.

Leaders, like companies, start with goals and aspirations for themselves, as organizations do for themselves. Most people and companies will do admirable work. The best leaders and companies are those that reflect their personal leadership brand and the company's brand promise in all they do. The great leaders and companies will clearly and consistently reflect the brand.

One of the biggest differentiators between good and great is the superior customer experience that is provided on a consistent basis. During every customer interaction your reputation is on the line.

Remember, as a leader, your customers are also the people in your care and supervision. They are your customers.

I hope as you read through this book, you will enjoy the stories, have some reflective moments, and continue to strengthen your leadership brand.

If you were to begin each of the following thoughts with either "Have I made" or "Do I," it might lead to some interesting conversations with yourself. If you were to use them for leadership self-evaluation, substitute "my people" for the word "customer."

- **My Priority Is Customer Satisfaction:** Whether on the phone, in person, or via electronic communication, genuinely interact and connect with customers; ensure a positive experience and exceed expectations.

- **Actively Listen to Customer Needs:** Consistently demonstrate to customers you are in tune with their needs and are operating in their best interest. Customers know what they want but may not always explain it in a manner that is clear to you. Therefore, it is important to utilize effective listening skills. If you do not understand a request, ask clear, positively articulated questions until you understand. Do not rush customers, allow them at their own pace to discuss what they need. Once customers have expressed their needs, confirm your understanding with them to ensure communication is clear.

- **Build Strong Relationships:** Providing value and listening are key components of any relationship. The foundation of strong relationships also includes being fair to customers and following through on your word. Make sure to ask for assistance from others when necessary to ensure proper follow-through and response. Treat every customer how you would like to be treated.

- **Learn the Products and Services:** Part of providing a superior customer service experience is being knowledgeable of the services that are offered. Take the time to really learn your business so you can effectively communicate to your customers the services and value you provide.

- **Be Responsive and Effectively Resolve Problems:** If a problem occurs, allow customers to fully explain the issue and convey empathy. If the fault lies with you or your organization, take ownership of it and apologize. Take the initiative to resolve problems in a timely and effective manner.

- **Remain Positive:** Always show respect for your customers even if you find yourself in a challenging situation. Demonstrate professionalism and keep communication positive.

- **Express Gratitude:** Expressing appreciation can go a long way. It can be as simple as thanking customers for their business and loyalty. Make sure they know we are grateful they choose to do business with us.

Creating a strong culture is critical to you and your company's long-term success and growth. It should be your desire and that of your organization to create the Best, Brightest, Most-Informed and Best-Educated management team in the industry.

In the service business, people are the most important asset. The time we spend with our people is an investment in the future, not an expense or burden on our time. You cannot successfully grow the business without an investment in people.

This is an important first step to building a performance culture. This investment will result in success for your company and personal and professional growth for you. You must view the business through the eyes of a leader. By the way, that's you.

Your success will be measured by the degree to which everyone in your organization at every level begins to understand, embrace, emulate, and execute the vision and strategy.

Good Luck, be safe, and remember

The Speed of the Leader Determines the Pace of the Pack

CONTENTS

CHAPTER 1

SIMPLE ACTS OF KINDNESS

Joe Scafone arrives at his seat and takes a deep breath as he begins to settle in for his long flight home from Orange County, California.

But before he can get comfortable, he cannot get past the gladiator event he just participated in, referred to as *"the boarding process."*

Scarred and battered from many years of the boarding process, Joe would just once love to meet the person who had the responsibility to map and design this process. If you subscribe to the theory that the purpose of process mapping and work flow diagrams is to bring forth a clearer understanding and communication of a process and then execute it at a high level consistently, then this process is clearly not working the way it was designed.

The boarding process to Joe and his frequent flyer friends is the definition of organized chaos. It is survival of the fittest or, better put, survival of the "firstest." It is all about getting to your seat early and claiming your spot.

The engineer who designed this process, he thought, *needs to be in the boarding process just once as a participant, to be a gladiator. To stand there in anticipation of the boarding announcement or better yet hearing the agent at the gate announce, "LET THE GAMES BEGIN" and to see it unfold, the huddled masses approaching the Jetway.*

The process starts out with good intentions and many directions but quickly devolves to chaos. Today was no different.

It started in its normal process.

"Good afternoon, passengers. This is the preboarding announcement for flight 1907 with service to Newark's Liberty International Airport."

But before the next sentence in the announcement begins, people and carry-ons are on the move.

The gate agent continues, "We are now inviting those passengers with small children and any passengers requiring assistance to board at this time. The first class cabin will begin boarding in ten minutes."

Seems simple, but too much is left to interpretation. At this point 80% of the flight is huddled around the agent's desk and at the opening of the Jetway. The games have begun and anticipation and anxiety fill the boarding area.

These announcements all sound good, but in reality, what do they literally mean? And more importantly, how do the boarding gladiators interpret them?

Well, based on the boarding processes we have all experienced, you need to prepare yourself to bump and grind your way onto the plane.

Joe reasoned, the plane and the processes associated with it are really a paradigm for life and business. People rationalize that there are rules, but these rules do not apply to them. These rules are for the 20%

of the people who have not moved yet or have not arrived at the gate.

When the agent announces, "Passengers with small children" this gets interpreted as, we were all children once, we are young at heart, or my 16-year-old acts like a child, so I can board at this point.

As a process-oriented, rules-following person, Joe spent a lot of time in his life and career shaking his head during these difficult and sometimes annoying events. He vowed to remain positive and always show respect for those around him. It was no different in his work environment. His commitment was the same: Treat his people and his customers with dignity and respect even when he found himself in these challenging situations.

The toughest part of his commitment at times was to demonstrate professionalism and always keep his communication positive. Joe was a "Jersey Guy," which meant he had an excellent grasp of sarcasm. The knowledge and ability to use it at a moment's notice challenged his personal commitment. The boarding process challenged his commitment and resolve.

Well enough on the boarding process, he thought, *time to settle in for the long ride home.*

Regardless of what the latest advertisements were professing about legroom and comfort, the fact remained that personal space is at a premium on an airplane.

Joe politely arranged his stuff and was ready to take his seat. As a businessman with more than 35 years of experience in the world of logistics, transportation, and old-fashioned people management, he believed thoughtfulness was an important trait of a good leader and essential in a good person.

He was also not a gear guy; he could not be bothered with nor did he choose to lug around a neck pillow, eye mask, or earplugs. He toyed with noise-canceling headphones but was more concerned with getting on board, placing his carry-on in the overhead and getting settled in than canceling noise.

He had a routine he had developed over his many years of flying that he proudly viewed as his "scientific and efficient approach to travel." As he was settling into his seat, he often wondered why his beautiful, practical, and far less neurotic wife Adrianne viewed his routine as obsessive-compulsive behavior that did not work with her personal travel routine.

Plan the Work, Work the Plan, he thought was always one of the ingredients for success.

He had just navigated the rental car return, serpenting his way through the security line with his new TSA Precheck status (Joe was not only a trusted leader and manager but now he was a trusted traveler) and boarding early with his premium status.

Flight 1907 was no ordinary flight for Joe. Unlike all his flights in the past, this one was different in one important way: this was his last flight as a business professional. He was heading home, this time with no flight or meeting scheduled for next week.

He had had a distinguished career, filled with new assignments, relocations, and many opportunities to learn new things, meet new people, and explore new geographies.

He looked forward to this flight as an opportunity to relax and reflect on this wonderful career.

Joe buckled his seat belt, turned off his cell phone, and sat back into his seat proud of the fact that he had accomplished his travel plan while still adhering to his personal rule that "a little consideration goes a long way."

At the beginning of his professional journey, his vision was simple; Joe aspired to be a high school history teacher and a baseball coach. He had envisioned himself instructing and empowering those around him.

Joe is a creature of habit (considered detail-oriented by some and obsessive-compulsive by others) and so everything he did was calculated, even the way he traveled. Any flight over two hours required Joe to be in an aisle seat, a risk some would say, considering the dangers of the beverage cart targeting the elbows and knees of the unaware aisle-seated passengers on board. Joe never wanted to be boxed in— on an airplane, in life, or in business. He was a forward thinker and always prepared.

But 35 years of business travel and the diamond status that came along with it meant Joe could always reserve exactly what seat he wanted. The armrest, on the other hand, was another story. The theory that says the passenger in the middle seat earns the right to both armrests because of the discomfort associated with the middle seat was not a theory Joe subscribed to. He had a fundamental issue with the theory of the armrest. It came down to numbers. Joe had a mathematical mind and was a natural at engineering solutions and problem solving. There is no pragmatic answer to four armrests for three passengers—it was survival of the fittest. If someone was going to win, why not him?

As the flight crew made its final preparations and passengers sent texts and emails before takeoff, Joe prepared himself for his fake sleep routine. Joe is a friendly guy, but by no means has he ever become fully comfortable on an airplane. He considered it a personal accomplishment that his rosary beads were now virtual instead of physically cupped in his right hand, while his prayer cards rested comfortably in the inside pocket of his suit.

A well-practiced fake nap allowed him the opportunity to compose himself, not to mention avoid a potentially forced awkward conversation or, even worse, idle chitchat. The overhead bins were closed; it was a full flight yet no one had sat to fill the middle seat next to him. Joe anxiously awaited the announcement that the boarding door had been closed. Would he be lucky enough to have the seat next to him empty or would his row be filled at the last minute, forcing him out of his routine and into the world of small talk?

Joe slowly raised his eyes and saw an elderly woman boarding— she appeared frightened and nervous. As she approached his row it was obvious that the armrest was the last thing on her mind. Joe politely greeted the woman, helped her with her carry-on luggage, and they settled into their seats.

Before he could close his eyes, the woman hit Joe with her elbow. "Hello," she said, "it is a pleasure meeting you. My name is Vincenza, but all my friends and family call me Nonna."

Joe smiles and introduces himself as Joe; she promptly and enthusiastically tells him that she has both a brother and a cousin named Giuseppe just like him.

Joe smiles, knowing that Giuseppe is his name in Italian. He is also grateful that with a name like Joseph, she hasn't asked him if he was a carpenter (although he is handy around the house). The flight attendants finish their preflight preparations as the two share pleasantries about being Italian. Joe thinks back to his childhood and the pleasant memories growing up Italian Catholic and how he regularly attended the Church of Our Lady of Perpetual Guilt.

As he closes his eyes, she taps him on the elbow. "I don't fly often and I am a little nervous," Nonna whispered.

Just as he is about to reassure her that he has flown many flights without incident, the pilot makes his announcement: "Welcome to flight 1907 en route to Newark's Liberty International Airport. Flight time is four hours and 45 minutes wheels up to touch down. I am your pilot, Antonio Aero, and your copilot on this flight is Tom Treno. Sit back and relax and enjoy the flight."

Joe turns to Nonna and says, "We are so lucky that Antonio is our pilot; he is one of the best! I've flown with him many times and it is always a safe, pleasant flight. I always hope that he is the pilot."

A calm comes over her face. This comment eased her fears. Joe thinks nothing of it, but simple gestures and acts of kindness are among the many traits that separate Joe from his peers. Joe believes that these selfless simple acts of kindness are part of the characteristics that inspire loyalty and motivate people to achieve levels of success that they never dreamed they could achieve. Someone had to believe in them before they were ready to believe in themselves.

The cockpit door closes, the walkway is slowly moved into position, and the jet starts its roll onto the ramp. A quiet comes over the plane and it seems most passengers succumb to their own routines. Even Nonna has peacefully closed her eyes in a quiet solitude knowing that Antonio is at the helm and Joe has great confidence in him.

THE LESSON:
SIMPLE ACTS OF KINDNESS.

> » Simple acts of kindness allow you to connect with your people on a human level, inspiring loyalty and instilling confidence.

> » They need someone to believe in them until they are ready to believe in themselves.

> » Effective coaching is an enabling process. It enables or inspires individuals to do more, which in turn enables or helps groups to perform better.

> » Treating your people, customers, and those around you in a thoughtful manner and with dignity and respect is an essential component of leadership. It is critical when you are in challenging situations.

CHAPTER 2
A SIGNIFICANT EVENT

The plane steadily climbs into the sky and the familiar ping startles some of the passengers who are not into a deep sleep. Joe knows an announcement is coming. The flight attendant goes into her memorized speech: "We have just passed through 10,000 feet on our way to our cruising altitude of 36,000 feet. You may now use your portable devices, and the Internet is available for purchase for those who wish to use it."

Joe has heard these announcements before, some so scripted he could repeat them chapter and verse. On some flights, the crew makes an effort to be more animated with their in-flight safety presentation and announcements to help ease the nervous energy of some of the passengers on board. For Nonna's sake, Joe was relieved this was a by-the-book crew.

Because even though he and some other frequent fliers may enjoy their vibrancy and attempt at humor, he did not think that Nonna's nerves would be able to handle it. It was a good thing Nonna was sleeping. The thought of hearing Antonio, her beloved pilot, over the intercom announcing, "Ladies and gentlemen, we have just reached our cruising altitude now, so I am going to turn off the fasten seat belt sign. You are free to move about the cabin, but please stay inside the plane until we land; it is quite cold out there. Weather in Newark is 50 degrees with broken clouds, but they should be fixed by the time we land. Sit back and relax and enjoy the flight to Newark" may not have amused Nonna or made her feel more comfortable.

Joe was not a sleeper on the plane: his time was calculated and he took great pride in his efficiency. The plane was a place to get things done. He reaches into his backpack at his feet and pulls out his portable device. He releases his tray table, and connects to the in-flight Internet. *Technology is a wonderful thing,* Joe thought. *I wonder if my parents felt the same way when they purchased their first TV or when their own personal telephone replaced the party line.* Joe did not always believe in technology. There was a time when technology was the skill he and his peers struggled to embrace and preferred to delegate. He would say it was a necessary evil left for the proverbial "smart guy" to figure out for them. Joe was from Jersey after all, where everybody had a "guy" and he would rely on the "guy" for all his technology needs.

Old-school thinking, he thought. In business as in life a significant moment or event is what propels people to change. Often the hardest part of the moment isn't the event itself but recognizing it as an event, or better yet a teaching moment. Technology was something that all leaders needed to embrace, understand, and master. Technology was the perfect example for Joe as he remembers the exact moment the "smart guy" theory would not be enough if he wanted to stay relevant in business and as a leader.

Joe and his wife, Adrianne, had been blessed with four beautiful children, as if they had put their order in: two girls and two boys. His family had moved many times over the years of his career—a few kicking and screaming. Adrianne was the happy matriarch of the family who always found a way to make each move an adventure and keep everyone grounded.

Their youngest child, Andrew Vincent, was struggling one school night with the concept of greater than and lesser than. It was a rare weeknight at home for Joe, who was usually traveling or attending a sporting event, a cheerleading or dance competition.

He was taking the opportunity to get caught up on the History Channel when Adrianne looked at him in her calm, collected but authoritative voice and said, "Now may be a good time to jump in and help, Dad."

Joe thought, *I have worked through some very complicated work problems and discussed ROIC (return on invested capital) like it was a family member. I got this.*

He said, "Andrew Vincent, let's talk about greater than and less than." After using many examples to no avail, he took three hockey pucks and put them on one side of the table and put four on the other and asked Andrew Vincent, "What does this mean?"

With a smile he answered, "We have seven hockey pucks."

Then Joe thought, *I got it!* He took out a piece of paper and drew the signs < (less than), and > (greater than), held up the paper and asked, "Andrew Vincent, what do these signs mean to you?"

Proudly he said, "Dad, that's easy—fast forward and reverse."

It was at that moment that Joe realized the world around him was changing. In this new world order, technology was going to be an important part of this change; it would be the new industrial science.

The future would be filled with new technologies, devices, and technical knowledge.

The next generation of people, employees, and leaders was going to be tech savvy, and technology would be second nature to them.

If Joe was going to lead and inspire them, he had better embrace technology. Joe would have to become "the guy!" Technology was here to stay and if Joe wanted to stay relevant, he needed to go where the puck was going, not where the puck had been.

In order to stay relevant and current as a leader, he would have to challenge himself to maximize his potential so he could inspire and maximize the potential of his employees. He would need to be more flexible and to be open to managing a diverse workforce in challenging and changing times.

As he thought through his significant event and moment with Andrew Vincent, he thought, *In today's world he would not have used paper to draw out greater than or less than, they would have just Googled it!*

The rumble of the beverage cart nearby brought Joe back from his "I got it" moment with Andrew Vincent. Joe went through the drill mechanically: tray down, knees and elbows in, and a snack choice of peanuts, pretzels, or biscotti cookies was the first decision to be made.

Just as the flight attendant was about to ask their choices, Nonna opened her eyes and with a big smile proclaimed, "Buon pomeriggio, come stai oggi?" Realizing the puzzled look on the flight attendant's face, she immediately replied, "Good afternoon, how are you today?"

A wide smile naturally crossed Joe's face at the sound of Nonna's beautiful Italian. It brought him back to his childhood, and family events chock full of all his aunts and uncles talking at once, reverting to their native Italian to better make their points. Wonderful memories.

It also highlighted to him a lesson he learned through 35 years of training workshops attended—one he had often repeated himself as an instructor.

What you learn first, you retain the longest.

That is, if at a moment's notice you are in a critical, high-pressure situation you will start with those things you learned first and remembered the longest. Nonna was the living proof of the theory.

In sports, it's often called muscle memory: you are what you practice and at that critical moment in a game you instinctively do what you have practiced over and over again.

Joe thought back to his days as a leader, mentor, and coach and asked himself, *Did I always start a new job or a new business relationship with an eye toward establishing first things first and making that good first impression that will be retained the longest?*

Toward the end of his career, Joe started a personal practice that, as he took on new roles and responsibilities, he would design and develop a 100-day plan, his road map. In this plan he scripted his vision, goals, and aspirations for his business, his people, and himself. By doing this, Joe could make that positive first impression and thoughtfully manage his customers, people, and stakeholders to a successful outcome.

Before he could get too deep into his thoughts, Nonna shrugged, "No espresso, but biscotti cookies?"

She smiled but seemed a little annoyed, yet took the cookies with the water. Joe was sure she thought it seemed a little odd, but it still seemed like a good snack.

After the flight attendant moved on, Nonna turned to Joe and reasoned, "They must have the biscotti cookies because Antonio must have requested them and not everyone likes espresso and they probably don't have any Anisette on the plane."

Joe nodded politely but couldn't stifle a good laugh. Memories are like that.

THE LESSON:

LEADERS GO TO WHERE THE PUCK IS GOING, NOT TO WHERE THE PUCK HAS BEEN.

» In business and in life, a significant moment or event is what propels people to change. Recognize those moments.

» Be "the guy" or "the gal" who is ready to put into action what they learned as they embrace new challenges. Get outside your comfort zone.

» Be the leader who motivates and inspires your people to do the best job they are capable of doing today and in the future.

CHAPTER 3
VALUES MATTER

Nonna looked at Joe and asked many questions about him and his family. She had been well schooled in the handbook of "Italian Grandmothers and Their Most Frequently Asked Questions." They always start out pleasant but—depending on your answers—can quickly move to too judgmental. Joe was prepared.

"Where are you from?" she asked.

"Well, I grew up in New Jersey, but I was born in New York," he responded.

"What parish?"

You see, when you tell someone you are from New Jersey, they usually respond, "What exit?" When you tell an Italian Catholic grandmother where you are from they ask, "What parish?" Joe told her he was baptized in Saint Anthony's and she gave him an approving smile. As Nonna moves through the handbook of questions, she realizes Joe has moved quite often.

With a tilt of the head and a compassionate look, she asks, "Is everything okay? You are not in some kind of trouble?" She continues, "It's okay, we all make mistakes. Have you been to confession or talked to your parish priest? I am sure he can help."

Joe reassures Nonna all is good and the moves were job related and all for good reasons.

She makes the sign of the cross and tells him, "Thank God. I knew you were a good boy."

Joe told her that he had just retired and was in fact on his way home to New Jersey from his last business meeting.

"I really look forward to enjoying my family and following my wife around the local food market," he said with a smile.

Before he could continue, she interrupted him. With a nervous smile she said, "It may not be as easy as declaring when you get home tonight, 'Honey I am home, what are we doing tomorrow?'"

Joe stopped and thought for a minute. He always fancied himself to be a lifelong learner and a planner but in this case he had done neither. Retirement was something he hadn't given a lot of thought to until this trip.

Meeting Nonna may not be a coincidence, he thought, *but a God-incidence.* She may be giving him one of the most important lessons as he started his new career—retirement! He realized he may have to develop a new plan and he certainly did not want to make a bad first impression on his first day of retirement.

Joe shared with Nonna stories about each of the moves—from the East Coast to the West Coast and back. She enjoyed hearing how the kids adjusted. As Nonna reached the end of the "handbook," her eyes seemed to be getting heavy, but she did have one more question: "What made you decide to move so often and were your parents okay with all of the moves?"

Joe stopped and thought for a moment. He had never intended to move often or even outside of the town where he grew up. So how did it happen? Joe had been very fortunate throughout his career to have the opportunity to work with, learn from, and mentor some incredible people. But no one was more influential in his early life than his family and parents—in particular his father. Nonna got a second wind when Joe started to talk about how it all started, his family, and the influences that led to the decisions that he made.

"I was born in New York City but raised in New Jersey. My father was born in Italy and moved to the United Sates at the age of 14."

Before Joe could continue, Nonna interrupted him. "Was he Neapolitan or Calabrese?" To Nonna this was an important question that had to be answered before she could move on.

"My father was Neapolitan and my mother was Calabrese." Nonna proudly smiled: she was Neapolitan and Calabrese also.

"Anyway, my mother was born in the U.S. but went back to Italy for some time before coming back to the States to live. I'm the oldest of four in a very traditional, old-fashioned Italian family. My dad stayed in high school only through his freshman year before leaving school and getting a full-time job as a tool and die maker in New York City. My mother did not work until later on, as my family had some illnesses that were expensive and necessitated my mother getting a job."

Nonna seemed to hang on every word.

"The town I moved to in New Jersey did not have a lot of Italians. Although we spoke Italian inside the house, when I was outside the house I only spoke English because my parents wanted our family to be American."

It was true. Although they were proud to be Italian, his father was very happy to be in the States, and very proud to be Italian American. Joe lived in the same two-family house his entire life until he moved out when he got married. They lived upstairs, and his aunt, uncle, cousin, and grandma lived downstairs.

They had a very family-oriented childhood and almost every weekend had relatives over the house. Joe's father instilled in all the children the values of hard work, integrity, and respect. Joe often thought (as he looked back and understood finances now as a husband and a parent) that growing up they were on the cusp of being poor, but never knew it. His parents and aunt and uncle never spoke about money or how tight things were, only that you have one family and make sure you take care of each other because nothing comes before or between you and your family.

Joe always believed that he was very fortunate to be raised in an environment where you were taught respect. You could disagree, but you were not allowed to be disagreeable or disrespectful. And he was taught that money did not motivate you, achievement did. The measure of your success was based on your success relative to your expectations. You achieved your success the old-fashioned way: you earned it through hard work.

So how did these influences get Joe and his family around the country and in eight different houses? It goes back to the conversation Joe had with his dad prior to his first job. As they sat around the kitchen table, and Joe was describing the job, his dad gave him advice that guided Joe throughout his career. His dad looked at him and calmly and in his own way said, "Joe, in everything you do, be the best you can be; you owe it to your family. Learn everything you can about your job, and then learn some more. Whatever they ask you to do say, 'Yes and thank you for the opportunity.'"

"So, Nonna," Joe said, "every time I was asked to move, I always thought back to my dad's advice and I said yes. My father believed you lived your values. Growing up, my father would emphasize, 'It is what you do when no one is watching that counts.'"

Nonna nodded her head, agreeing with Joe's wisdom from his father. It all came down to integrity. Joe, over his career, believed in not only the integrity of your word but the integrity of your actions as well, and the two were equally significant and important. Most people can relate to the integrity of one's actions. You act professionally. You refrain from taking what's not yours. As time went on and technology became a bigger factor in today's busy world, Joe began to think integrity of one's word (both written and spoken) was often overshadowed.

To Joe, integrity of one's word simply means to make a commitment and keep it. Do what you say. Be accountable to yourself and others. Follow up when you say you will. Promptly return phone calls and reply to emails. These small actions add up to great value.

Nonna looked at Joe and with great pride, as if he was her own son, said, "Your family and father especially must be very proud of you."

"Thanks for the kind words," Joe said, assuring her that his father was very proud of all of his children and each had their place in his heart.

She nodded as a proud parent herself and said, "I am sure you have many lessons from your career that you have shared with the many people you have worked with and touched." With that Nonna drifted off, settling in for the flight. Joe on the other hand wondered, *What is my legacy and what are the stories that will be repeated about me?*

THE LESSON:

VALUES MATTER. IT TAKES COURAGE
OF YOUR CONVICTION TO MAKE IT
THROUGH THE LONG HAUL.

» Leaders live their values and set the tone from the top.

» Leaders can disagree and are often challenged to find the better way. Live by the rule: you can disagree, but you should not be disagreeable or disrespectful.

» Be humble and learn everything you can about your job, and then learn some more.

» Recognize it is what you do when no one is watching that counts most because it's the true measure of your character.

CHAPTER 4
THE LEADERSHIP EQUATION

Joe did have many stories and some, over the years, had taken a life of their own. Adrianne often said the reason Joe needed to move often in his career was to get a new audience. She had heard them all after 35 years of marriage. Joe did have favorite or signature stories that over time defined his management style and leadership strategy. Some stories were just experiences and interactions with the wonderful people he and his family had met along the way during their many moves.

Joe got the call for a promotion and moved to the Hawkeye State. Their new address would be just outside the capital city of Des Moines, Iowa. As a kid growing up in New Jersey, and not paying much attention in geography, Joe thought west of the Mississippi was Pittsburgh. As he grew in the world of logistics and transportation, his geography got much better. This was not true for the family. They spent many hours researching and trying to understand where Iowa was and how long it took to drive there.

Joe took great pride and time to travel around the state, meet the people, and see the places they did business in. He could answer the question from the movie *Field of Dreams* without hesitation. "Is this Heaven? No, it's Iowa!"

Joe and his family were regulars at the Iowa State Fair and visited the many wonderful attractions in the state such as the Bridges of Madison County and the Pella Tulip Festival and enjoyed the rivalry between Iowa and Iowa State University.

He enjoyed letting his fellow Iowans know that he knew Johnny Carson was born in Corning and lived in Iowa throughout his early years. Shawn Johnson, Olympic gymnast and gold medalist, was born and raised in Des Moines. Herbert Hoover, our 31st president, was born in West Branch, Iowa, and John Wayne, the Duke's, birthplace is Winterset, Iowa. Just to name a few fun facts.

Joe thought nothing of it; he enjoyed his many visits and learning experiences and naturally walked the talk from a business leadership perspective. Joe fondly remembers the number one question people would ask him after they heard his name was Joe Scafone and the fact he was from New Jersey: "Are you in the witness protection program?"

Joe would always smile and answer, "No, but, if I was, my name would probably be Joe Smith, not Joe Scafone."

Joe loved these encounters and meeting the people in the new locations and his business operations. He took great pride in learning as much as he could about the people and their state. Joe always felt it was a sign of respect. He could never understand how peers would move into a new environment and then spend all their time critiquing the place and the people. He believed that would be like walking into someone's house and critiquing their taste in furniture. It may not be his style or taste, but why criticize theirs?

Joe's lessons on respect, leadership, and integrity from his dad went deep and wide, and as time has gone on they have become part of his own mantra and style. Imitation is the greatest form of flattery, after all, and his hope was that there was someone imitating his thoughts on respect, leadership, and ways to treat customers and associates.

Joe's dad had passed away more than eight years ago, after a struggle with cancer. Through a difficult time, Joe's dad never lost his dignity and respect for others. His gentle smile and comforting eyes were his signature style to the end. Joe often wondered, if asked by his dad, how would he describe his leadership style and strategy? What made his son tick? What was the difference between his son and all the rest?

Joe took out a piece of paper and a pen and thought, *It's time for old school—let's write it down.* He thought back to an early workshop where the instructor had the class write their eulogy as part of an exercise. He thought maybe this was the approach he would take to answer the question if they had had this conversation before his dad had passed.

As Joe has often stated both publicly and privately, he has been very fortunate through his career to have the opportunity to work with and learn from some incredible people. While they all came from different walks of life, they did have some traits and skills and beliefs that made them more similar than dissimilar. Although he did not profess to be smarter than anyone else or an expert, he had been shaped and influenced by some outstanding people at all levels. He also had a family that was a great influence but also had a way of keeping him grounded.

He began to write his traits, attributes, and skills on the paper. Really, he began to write the story of Joe Scafone in the manner in which he would have told his dad. Joe, like his dad, believed it starts with values. It is what you do when no one is watching that counts. Integrity can often be used to describe this activity, but he took it further. It is integrity of your word as well as your actions.

Joe also believed that two fundamental ingredients of a success-ful person that were part of his success equation are hard work and enthusiasm. There is no substitute for hard work and an equation that he used was Time + Effort + Enthusiasm = Results. Enthusiasm is what fuels your drive and keeps the engine revving. Without enthusi-asm your equation is time and hard work, and although these are two important ingredients to success, Joe never lost sight that hard work without enthusiasm is just that: HARD WORK. Hard work by itself gets old without enthusiasm.

Another way Joe looked at it was "Make it Fun but Make it Happen." Finally, he believed we should all ask ourselves some key questions and answer them with a critical eye and with honesty of purpose. How can I add value in this current position and going forward? Do I have a process mind with a strategic vision and the ability to execute the strategy tactically? Can I develop a strategy, build a business plan, and execute that plan? Can I provide clear communication and walk the talk? Can I teach my teams to learn to take better control of their day and balance multiple priorities, measuring and following up for con-tinuous improvement? Do I accept the responsibility for my results? Do I have the ability to effectively assess

- who I am
- what I stand for
- what I will never compromise?

Although his dad may not have described it this way, Joe took great pleasure in the knowledge that his dad would have understood and respected who Joe had become, the skills he had learned, and the ques-tions Joe would ask himself. He believed, after writing it down, his dad would have been proud of his accomplishments. His father would be proud of the fact that Joe's description of a leader and the traits he aspired to lead with were inspiration, motivation, training, and development of his people. Great leaders get people and organizations to attain success beyond what they would have done on their own. There is no doubt his father had done this for him and his family.

Thoughtful leaders are strong during the difficult times and know when to discipline, when to celebrate, and when to be in the background. They are humble, thoughtful, and bring energy and enthusiasm to their role. Joe would hope that people would view him this way and his eulogy would reflect this.

Joe placed the pen on the tray and took a deep breath. These were the moments when he missed his dad the most. It was not at the family functions as most had thought. Joe knew he would not be there. Joe missed the conversations like this one, the ones where he would be sharing a special family moment. These were the most heartbreaking. Joe did take great comfort that his dad was looking down, sitting at a giant kitchen table with many of the relatives and friends that had passed. He pictured his dad with a smile, talking about his family and maybe Joe and Joe's accomplishments. Joe also knew it would not be too long into the conversation before he would ask him, "Joe, why do you need so many TVs? Who are you trying to impress? That is not who we are and where we came from."

Joe translated these conversations and that question into valuable lessons that had gotten him through the many ups and downs, days and nights during a long career.

Don't let your highs get too high or your lows get too low. Make sure you can put your head on your pillow at night knowing that you were a good person that people respected and don't get caught up in your success. Be humble, let other people sing your praises. Joe would get back to the eulogy, but nature was calling and Joe needed a break.

THE LESSON:

ENTHUSIASM IS WHAT FUELS YOUR DRIVE
AND KEEPS THE ENGINE REVVING.

» Great leaders get people and organizations to attain success beyond what they would have done on their own through a profound commitment to putting forth the time, effort, and enthusiasm needed to achieve results.

» Thoughtful leaders are strong during the difficult times. They know when to discipline, when to celebrate, and when to be in the background.

» Don't let your highs get too high or your lows get too low. Maintain your balance.

CHAPTER 5

TAKING CARE OF BUSINESS

Joe collected himself and looked up and down the aisle to assess the lines and his strategy for his bathroom break and a much-needed stretch of his legs.

Although he was not far from the ominous and imposing curtain that separated first class, Joe was a "rules guy" so he quickly eliminated the thought of being a rebel with a cause and using the first class rest rooms, or (as they call them in the air) lavatories.

As a rules guy, he started his walk to the back. As he made his way to the back, he was struck with the phenomenon that has become the new world order. A light show on an airplane. The shades had all been pulled down to create what was in the past a restful place to sleep. Although he did observe some people sleeping, the vast majority were all deep into their hand-held devices, phones, iPads, and tablets. They had created a light show that would rival a concert.

Joe and Adrianne had just had a conversation at dinner this past weekend as they sat at a restaurant and noticed that the kids at most of the tables were deep into their Game Boys and smart toys. Technology had become the babysitter.

Adults were checking their text messages or Googling some fact. Sadly, very few were deep into conversation as a family or couples or just friends enjoying time together.

Joe always spoke to his people about his belief that you always have to make sure that "your strength does not become your weakness." He critiqued himself often on this principle and held himself to this same standard.

He would often cite an example using himself. His strength was his energy, passion, and enthusiasm. This at times was also his weakness. This energy, passion, and enthusiasm sometimes did not allow him to listen intently, or he would run past others in his zeal.

Companies and organizations have the same issue. A company's strength may be their processes and procedures. This may also be their weakness if it does not allow them to be open to change or adjustments to changing times and commitments.

Technology was certainly a strength: e-commerce, the Internet, and social media were all exciting breakthroughs. In applying the test of not allowing your strength to become your weakness, technology could also become a weakness when it came to social interactions. The simple face-to-face conversation, or note written to say thank you, was becoming a thing of the past. The personal touch was still an important asset in business, both as a person and leader.

A few were taking advantage of the time to get things done and he aligned himself with this crowd. As he was deep into his thoughts, a young boy tapped him on the back and asked if he was in line for the bathroom. He politely replied yes but said he could go first if he wanted to. With a big smile the boy thanked him and passed on by.

As Joe walked back to his seat, consumed with this thought of technology and personal interactions, he was, however, impressed from a historical perspective with how far we have come.

In fact, it was not too long ago that Joe and Adrianne were having a conversation with their children about getting beepers (also known as pagers). One of Joe's stories that he loved to tell, which was not as funny to Adrianne, went back to the beeper era and their third relocation.

Joe worked at being a good communicator and the events of the day helped him to complete a lesson or make a point as part of a teaching moment. The high school history teacher in him always came out at some point.

His view started with the belief that to be a good communicator you first need to understand your role as a leader—what you do as well as what's expected of you.

Second, it is important to understand and embrace your values and ethics and make sure they align with those of your organization. This alignment is critical for your credibility as a leader and will support your style because you will be comfortable in who you are and what you stand for.

Third, you need to use and develop a reliable process for communicating that fits your style. For most people this means acquiring, practicing, and using a set of communication skills that allows you to communicate clearly, comfortably, and effectively with employees, peers, your manager, and customers.

For him, his style clearly utilized storytelling, humor, and family events to communicate, teach, and describe the lessons and points he would be making. For him, email was no substitute for the personal interaction.

These stories that centered around trials, tribulations, and accomplishments were important tools to train and develop the people in his care and over the years had allowed both Joe and his people to gain the confidence and competence to successfully manage their day and perform their task. He would challenge each of them to develop their stories, their *Red Badges of Courage.*

In describing Adrianne, he had his stories. Some would say that this could be dangerous territory to venture into, but not for Joe.

Adrianne had her own style and routine. Joe and Adrianne met in college the first day of her freshman year. She was a very pretty, petite girl who got his attention the minute he saw her on campus. She was born and raised in Brooklyn, New York, and very proud of it. Like Joe, she was 100% Italian, so he was comfortable she knew the rules.

As he drove home, thinking about this wonderful new girl he had met, he thought she was pretty, a little shy, but when she spoke she had a bubbly personality, definitely someone he would like to date, but can she cook?

Would her sauce be thick or runny and her meatballs, ah her meatballs, could they be anything like his grandmother's?

Well, as you can see, she could cook, made great meatballs, and they were married and blessed with four beautiful children.

He often would describe her as E. F. Hutton. E. F. Hutton & Company was an American stock brokerage firm founded in 1904 by Edward Francis Hutton and his brother Franklyn Laws Hutton. Under their leadership, Hutton became one of the most respected financial firms in the United States and for several decades was the second largest brokerage firm in the United States.

So why did he refer to her as E. F. Hutton? Well, it was for more than the obvious of being one of the most respected firms with a leadership role in the financial community. It was because of what E. F. Hutton became best known for. The firm was best known for its commercials in the 1970s and 1980s based on the phrase "When E. F. Hutton talks, people listen."

Well, when Mom spoke, everyone listened, including Dad. Her style was not flashy, but she knew the right things to say at exactly the right time. She held the family together through all of the moves and growing pains of four children on the move.

She made each move an adventure, a new beginning, and it always started with her taking the lead. Her routine started with her driving in and around the new area and getting to know the people and the geography. She wanted to know what made this new place special so she could embrace it. Since this was all before GPS, her nickname became Rand McNally; she had a map in her hands at all times.

As her first act of business, she would go to a bowling alley, introduce herself, and get on a team that needed a bowler. Once she started to bowl, her 170 or better average made her an instant hit with the team. Her warm smile and inviting personality allowed her to make friends in the neighborhood quickly and easily. With four kids, the bus stop was a great place to start, and it wasn't long before she became part of the group.

It would not be long before she would tell Joe and the family about a neighborhood event where everyone was getting together. She always volunteered to help and participate in some manner. The kids were excited, but Joe was wondering, *Why are we getting to know all of these people when we are going to move again and then have to say goodbye?* Of course, Joe lost those discussions.

So on to the Beeper Story:

This event was a neighborhood block party and Joe was now learning that most of the neighbors were doctors of some sort. Joe tried hard to mingle and start conversations, but he was not met with much of a reception. As doctors, each of them had a beeper that they prominently displayed on their belt; each was better than the next.

Joe thought that without a beeper he had no street credibility. He went home and took his garage door opener, hooked it to his belt, and proceeded back out to the block party.

As he mingled, a few of the neighbors were looking at his garage door opener with a puzzled look. Joe proudly responded, "International beeper."

Joe broke the ice and spent the rest of the day getting to know the neighbors and the garage door opener became the conversation of the day. That night, Joe looked at his family and said that was a nice time. They all looked at each other, smiled, and thought Grandpa would say, "Who are they trying to impress?" He smiled and thought, *That is exactly what he would say.*

Joe often spoke about the unintended consequences of decisions and actions. In this case the unintended consequence of the beepers was that the beepers set up a barrier to communication between Joe and the new neighbors. Once Joe broke the barrier with his garage door opener the dialogue began. Leaders must ensure there are no barriers to communication—real or perceived. They should listen with the intent to act on what they learn and invite feedback. This inspires openness and trust.

THE LESSON:
LEADERS MUST ENSURE THERE ARE
NO BARRIERS TO COMMUNICATION.

» Develop a reliable process for communicating that fits your style.

» To be a good communicator you first need to understand your role as a leader, what you do, as well as what's expected of you.

» To inspire openness and trust, listen with the intent to act and invite feedback. Articulate a clear set of organizational values that embrace integrity, fairness, and compassion.

» Values communicate beliefs.

» Thoughtful leaders listen and act on what they learn. This honesty and openness inspires trust, reinforces relationships, and secures the loyalty of employees, customers, and investors.

» Good communication is vital in a business environment marked by uncertainty and change and promotes healthy relationships.

CHAPTER 6
TIGHTEN THE LUG NUTS

Joe was in the moment as he reminisced and played back in his mind that story. As he thought through it again, it brought a smile to his face. If Adrianne had been sitting next to him on the flight and saw that smile and knowing he was in one of his moments, she would have responded, "It's amazing how you crack yourself up!"

Unfortunately, there was no time to bask in the memory. The flight was approaching the restless point. This is where flyers take out the unwritten handbook for flying entitled, "The Handbook for Flight Coping Mechanisms." The coping mechanisms were kicking in for some on this flight.

Long flights can be tough, so some passengers begin to use the airplane as their personal gym. Simple stretching exercises to relieve stress and improve circulation is perfectly acceptable. But trying to do yoga and other exercises in the aisle or back of the plane is another.

Another passenger heading to the back has completely removed their shoes and socks and is wearing what could be their pajamas. They have taken the theory of wearing comfortable clothes to a whole new level.

A few rows over is the man who has the ability to sleep on the plane but not the ability to control or understand his snoring. These are just a few of the coping mechanisms you will see on a flight.

Joe loves all of the sights and sounds. He is a people watcher at heart. He never takes himself too seriously. He never got too caught up in titles and levels and most would say that this may be his greatest quality. This is what has kept him grounded and approachable. His dad always had a way of keeping him and the family grounded. Adrianne now does a great job in performing that role for him as well.

People would often describe Joe as someone who was as comfortable in the C-suite as he was on the shop floor.

True to form and a creature of habit, he had just told the pager story in his last official meeting. He used it from a teaching perspective on communication and barriers. How we communicate and act is often how we garner people's respect and trust.

Leaders understand that they must be adaptive to their changing environments. The environment has certainly changed over the past 35 years. Sometimes you must simplify the message and other times you may have to be more creative and engaging.

Understanding the audience and being able to read the audience is an important skill that a successful communicator must perfect. If people look confused, ask for their feedback or confirmation. This will help you to understand if they understand the message, mission, assignment, and expectation.

There is no substitute for follow-up. Follow-up can be in a simple phone call or in a visit a few days later. This follow-up will also demonstrate your passion. As a leader and communicator you must inspire others. Nothing says you care about your message more than that personal follow-up touch.

Two other traits of a great communicator are being approachable and being prepared to listen. To Joe, nothing says "I am approachable" like walking around. Being prepared to listen can sometimes be difficult, but great leaders make the time to listen and solicit feedback. Soliciting feedback gets the runner on base; doing something with the feedback scores the run.

One of Joe's signature stories only happened because of this quality and belief. The story starts with Joe performing one of his favorite activities, walking the shop floor and talking with everyone he comes in contact with. Joe was a firm believer that leaders, at all levels, must encourage open and honest communications across, up, and down the organization, and especially with senior leadership.

As a leader, he knew he must articulate a clear set of organizational values that embrace integrity, fairness, and compassion. Values, he reasoned, are not the same as ethical guidelines or codes of conduct. Guidelines and codes are specific rules about what we can and cannot do. Values, on the other hand, are more profound and enduring. Values communicate beliefs. Walking the talk communicates these beliefs.

Joe always wanted his people to see the vision for the organization and believe in it. It also needed to be a vision that recognizes that a company has a purpose as part of a larger community as well. The best companies are passionate about contributing to society—from the products they sell to the examples they set and the causes they support. The best companies have a vision that employees are proud of, that customers believe in, and their people understand.

To do this, Joe believed there was not a better way to lead than by example—to be visible, available, and approachable. Joe also viewed these walks as personally therapeutic.

Joe began his walk on this particular day with great enthusiasm and with a purpose. It had been brought to his attention that this operation was deficient in a critical reporting element that pertained to its fleet of vehicles. Angelo Carro was the automotive supervisor in the building and was a high potential supervisor candidate. He had all the traits of hard work and enthusiasm. He was highly motivated, committed, and wanted to please. Joe thought he would seek him out on his walk and present this challenge to him. Joe's approach to Angelo was going to be simple: one building was going to be the best at this reporting element, why not yours?

Along the way, Joe spoke with all of the people in the building he came across. Ann was the building manager—she was recently promoted and was someone whom people respected. She was very approachable and her people knew they could talk to her. In this way she created an uncompromising culture of integrity, honesty, respect, and service. She embodied the open-door policy.

As Joe was approaching Angelo, he noticed that one of the vehicles on the line had loose lug nuts. He walked over to the vehicle and turned the lug nuts to see if he was correct and it was not an illusion. Sure enough, they were loose. Joe walked over to Angelo, greeted him warmly and said, "Angelo, I have a very important job to get done and I have great faith and confidence in you to do it."

"We need a rabbit," Joe was often heard to say. "The speed of the leader determines the pace of the pack." Joe told Angelo, "You are our person. But before I explain to you this critical job, the first vehicle on line one has loose lug nuts on the driver's side."

Angelo nodded and then asked, "Sir, what is it you need me to do? I am your guy."

Joe smiled back and explained, "We are having a problem with the daily vehicle inspection reports. It is important that we get this corrected and we need one operation to take the lead and show it can be done. I believe you can be that leader." Then Joe gave Angelo one of his favorite lines: "Someone is going to be the best at it. Why not you?"

Angelo accepted the challenge and told Joe, "I will not let you or the organization down."

Joe shook Angelo's hand and told him he would check in with him in a few days. Angelo left with great energy, enthusiasm, and purpose.

A few days later, Joe decides to take his walk and check in with Angelo. He looks around and does not see him on the floor talking with the drivers as he usually does. Joe asks a group of managers if they have seen him and they tell him he is in his office and that he had a road call emergency today. Joe walks in, greets everyone, looks around, and sees Angelo on the phone with a troubled look on his face.

As he hangs up the phone, he sees Joe for the first time.

Joe greets him and says, "I was coming by to see how you were doing on our project, but I heard you had an emergency road call to take care of this morning."

"I have had no luck," Angelo says, frustrated. "I was putting together my thoughts and approach when I received a call late last night on a road call that I have been working on all night and into this morning. One of our drivers at their first stop had their front driver side tire become so loose it could not be driven. Besides getting it fixed I had to arrange to get all the merchandise moved to make service. I have had no luck and I did not need this aggravation or headache."

Joe looked at Angelo and calmly but sternly asked, "Is this the vehicle I pointed out to you the other day with the loose lug nuts?"

Angelo thought and said, "Yes, it is."

Joe asked in a puzzled voice, "Why didn't you tighten the lug nuts after we spoke? At that moment it would only have taken you a few minutes to tighten the lug nuts."

Angelo responded, "You told me you had a very important job for me—I got caught up in fixing the important problem."

Joe looked at Angelo and told him, "This might be one of the most important lessons of your career and in life. You can only handle a few urgent things as a leader and in life. When you allow important things to become urgent you get overwhelmed. You can only handle and juggle a few urgent things. Tightening the lug nuts was important when I first spoke to you about it. Now it is urgent. The daily vehicle reports were important, but soon they will become urgent. The loose lug nuts you did not tighten when they were important and easy to fix are now preventing you from working on the reports, and soon this project will move from important to urgent."

Although he felt frustrated and embarrassed, that day Angelo became a disciple of Tightening the Lug Nuts and an Accountability Owner. He demonstrated an obligation or willingness to accept responsibility for his actions. This willingness to "own" the work results for him and his team began to separate him from his peers.

Completing your assigned work schedule on time and on budget takes planning and timely tightening of the lug nuts in your area of responsibility. These plans must be understood so you can recognize the important items that cannot be left for another time or day.

Each person in the organization from the supervisor to the CEO is accountable to make their business plan and pull their weight. Successful results come from all functions making their goals, whether those goals involve safety, service, people, or finances, and from not jeopardizing the results due to loose lug nuts caused by you or your team.

Joe kept in touch with Angelo over the years and he became a successful manager and leader because he had the ability to learn and grow from his challenges. Joe would often describe him after telling the story as a job developer possessing some excellent skills:

- First and foremost, as a supervisor you need to train your employees so they have both the confidence and competence to successfully manage their day and perform their tasks.
- You also need to acquire a set of coaching skills that help you both assess and reinforce acceptable behaviors and skills and achieve your work group's goals.
- Recognizing you might have some employees who are having difficulty meeting their job requirements, you also need to be prepared to provide targeted coaching to a challenging employee to obtain the desired behavior.
- Finally, *Tighten the Lug Nuts.*

THE LESSON:

LOOSE LUG NUTS DO NOT RELEASE PRESSURE; THEY INCREASE THE PRESSURE. TIGHTEN THE LUG NUTS TO PREVENT IMPORTANT THINGS FROM BECOMING URGENT!

» You can only handle a few urgent things, so do not allow important things to become urgent.

» Lead by example. Be visible, available, and approachable.

» Take the approach that someone is going to be the best, so why not you and your team? Make sure you are tightening lug nuts in your control as you lead by example.

» Work to acquire a set of coaching skills that help you both assess and reinforce acceptable behaviors and skills to achieve your work group's goals.

» We learn and grow from our challenges.

CHAPTER 7
LOOSE LUG NUTS SINK PLANS

Joe looked over to check in on Nonna: she was still asleep. He drifted back into his lug nut story and thought about how often he had used it and how powerful such a short story could be.

Lug nuts, he thought, came in all shapes and sizes, but all had one thing in common: if you didn't tighten them you will have problems. His dad would often say there are two things you can always count on happening in life: dying and paying taxes.

Joe had three you could count on: dying, paying taxes, and loose lugs nuts leading to problems.

As Joe turned on his laptop, his screen saver pictured Joe and Adrianne's first grandchild, Nico Anthony. This little boy, he thought to himself, has brought great joy to the family and was making the thought of retiring so much easier for him to embrace.

As he was thinking about all of the wonderful things they wanted to do and experience with Nico, Joe felt a tap on his arm: Nonna? As he turned to address her, he planned to show her the picture of Nico, but much to his surprise, it was not Nonna tapping his arm but the passenger sitting in the window seat. His arm was stretched across Nonna to reach him and with a smile he said, "Hello. I couldn't help but overhear as we were settling in that you are from New Jersey. I am traveling there on business and I am wondering if you could help me with some information."

Despite all of the different ways to communicate via technology, Skype, and video conferencing, there is still no substitute for meeting in person. Whether you are a young professional or seasoned business professional, business travel will be a part of your routine.

Joe's newest introduction was no different. He was a well-dressed business professional ready to hit the streets upon arrival. Joe had boarded before his newest acquaintance and traveler in arms. Although Joe did not know him personally, all indications were that he was a member of the Legion of Travelers. He carried the standard and appropriate carry-on and placed it in the overhead compartment quickly and effectively.

People have often asked Joe why he is always dressed for a flight and why he doesn't check a bag to avoid the hassle and anxiety of making sure there is space for his carry-on. The answer is simple: if the bag is lost or misrouted then Joe would be attending the meeting as the only person not dressed properly. He could not take that chance.

Like most frequent flyers, he had mastered packing and it was a science. A well-packed carry-on easily holds enough clean clothes for a week and he could not envision the disruption to his schedule that the wait at baggage claim can cause to a person on a mission and a tight schedule.

Joe's newest introduction exhibited all the traits of a seasoned flyer: proper suitcase, well-dressed, and a laptop case that carried all of the essentials for keeping him productive during his flight.

Joe politely responds, "Sure. What do you need?"

The man explains, "I did not get around to scheduling a service to pick me up at the airport so I could get to my destination in Central Jersey. Also, I am meeting a colleague who is flying into Philadelphia and I told her I would find a place for us to have dinner tonight in preparation for an early-morning meeting tomorrow. Do you have any suggestions for my travel to the hotel and dinner in the area?"

Joe looked at the gentlemen and said, "I think I can help." Feeling a kinship, he continued, "Don't you just hate the last-minute business trip? It has a way of disrupting your entire schedule both personally and professionally. They are the worst."

The gentlemen said, "I agree. I avoid the last-minute trips like the plague." He then proceeded to tell Joe, with an embarrassed look on his face, that this trip, however, had been planned for the last two months. He just got tied up with some other things and time got away from him.

A disappointing feeling overcomes Joe and he loses his feeling of kinship and camaraderie. He thinks to himself, *Sadly another loose lug nut has now caused this seasoned professional to allow important items to become urgent and he is about two hours from landing.*

He thought, *Nothing takes the wind out of your sails, or in this case, your plans, like procrastination.* Or as Joe calls them, *loose lug nuts.*

Joe proceeds to tell him that he has an excellent service that he uses and recommends, Chris Limousine Service, run by an excellent owner and entrepreneur named Paul.

The man nods his head in approval but then asks, "How long do you think it will take them to get to the airport to pick me up? I don't have a lot of time from touchdown to the time I told my colleague I would meet her for dinner. I hope these people are good!"

As Joe is listening to his questions it is difficult for him not to pass judgment. Joe was known to wear his emotions on his sleeve and his facial expressions were easily read. At times this was a detriment in his career and a killer at the poker table. He had worked hard on this over the years and had become much better at controlling these emotions. This was a change in behavior he had become proud of.

As he fights to keep his disapproval from appearing on his face and in his tone, he thinks to himself, *You are in this situation because you did not tighten the lug nuts and now you are concerned that things may not go smoothly and looking for someone to blame it on. Your problem isn't the car service or anyone else; the problem is you did not tighten the lug nuts when it was important and now it is urgent.*

But a wiser, older Joe stops short from introducing him to New Jersey sarcasm, and in the back of his head he hears his mother saying, "Joe, be nice." Joe then presented him with a few options for dinner. The man smiled and thanked him for his help.

Joe leaned back and thought back to the lug nut story. He has seen this movie many times and it does not end well. The ending is the same whether in business or in life: as things move from important to urgent, people begin to get overwhelmed.

Then the most discouraging part of the story takes place. Instead of taking ownership of the problem they caused by not tightening the lug nuts when it was important, now they take the role of the victim as it moves to urgent. It is never their fault: it is luck, fate, timing, their boss, anything but them. Joe wishes the man well and quickly returns to his laptop before he moves into a lecture on lug nuts and self-accountability.

Joe thinks to himself, *The lug nut story and procrastination have a lot in common.* We have all heard the saying "Never put off until tomorrow what you can do today." It reminds Joe of a story that he believes summarizes this point.

A good friend's father had passed away after a long, wonderful life in the town where they grew up. As his friend is going through his father's things in the attic he finds an old sport coat. In the pocket is a repair ticket for a pair of shoes his dad had dropped off at the shoemaker over 40 years ago. The shoemaker is still located on Main Street. He is in his late 80s as well, but still alive and in business at that same location. He wonders if the shoes are still there 40 years later or if his Dad had picked them up. After a few weeks, he musters up the courage to check it out. He walks into the shoe shop, greets the shoemaker, and hands him the ticket. The shoemaker looks at the ticket and walks to the back of the store.

After a few minutes, he returns and says, "They will be ready a week from Thursday."

Time is that precious commodity that we can never get back or buy more of. Time is similar to the old adage "We never get a second chance to make a good first impression." You never get a second chance to use the time you do not spend wisely or postpone using.

THE LESSON:
NEVER ALLOW THINGS TO AFFECT YOU
MORE THAN YOU CAN AFFECT YOURSELF.

- » As things move from important to urgent, people begin to get overwhelmed.

- » Tightening the lug nuts in a timely fashion ensures an efficient use of time and minimizes the number of urgent balls to juggle.

- » It allows you the opportunity to be the architect of your own destiny.

CHAPTER 8
BALANCED LEADERSHIP

Joe thought back to the eulogy exercise and how he would describe himself. He thought another good starting point was to capture his thoughts on leadership and what makes a good leader. He needed to write with a purpose; after all, he had less than two hours to go.

Joe believes the definition of a successful leader can be summarized as "a person who adds immediate value as a trusted advisor, mentor, and visionary." A leader is someone who uses a process approach to lead the organization and its people to new levels of success.

Great organizations need to have a thoughtful vision and strategy. Great leaders need to combine that strategic vision with the ability to tactically execute the strategy. That sounded good he thought, but there was more to it.

He added, a leader's vision and strategy must match the organization's vision and strategy and how it corresponds to what your associates, customers, and investors believe to be the company's strategy and vision. They must all be aligned. In today's economy, companies need to deliver advanced technologies and solutions with operational excellence through dedicated people who are the best, brightest, most informed and best educated in their industry.

Joe thought, *There are a lot of good business professionals out there. What makes him different? How would he describe this difference in his style and approach to leadership? Do my approach and results take me from good to great? Finally, what separates me from my peers?*

Now it became personal. He wanted to be remembered as a successful leader who thoughtfully managed his businesses based on the principles of Balanced Leadership.

Balanced Leadership was Joe's approach to business leadership; it was Joe's game plan. Joe believed it was important to view the business through the eyes of the three key constituents. He believed all three needed to be represented in all decisions that were made. Depending on the problem, one of the three may take the lead, but all three constituents needed a seat at the decision-making table. Who are they, and how did Joe address them?

To Joe it was simple. As you approach each problem and opportunity, you do it through the eyes of your customers, people, and stakeholders. Balanced Leadership is where each of us

- **Thinks like a customer** by approaching each challenge as a true solutions provider. We consider the business from the eyes of the customer and this guides our decisions and actions.
- **Feels like a valued individual** by knowing your work and your team's work matters and never compromising on safety. When you feel valued, you are empowered. You make smart decisions. You know you can talk to your manager and ensure your people know they can talk to you. By doing so, you create an

uncompromising culture of integrity, honesty, respect, and service. Joe believed he embodied the open-door policy by being approachable and in this way ensuring that he or his people never placed themselves in a compromising position.

- **Acts like an owner** by understanding the business and your role in what leads to success. When you consider the business as if it's your own, you pay careful attention to all of the above—your customers and people—and more. You take ownership of the problems as well as the results.

Owners, Joe rationalized, took care of the details. Joe believed in his Balanced Leadership approach and he had had great success with it throughout his career. He believed that Balanced Leadership gave him and his teams the opportunity to accurately comprehend the big picture. It gave them the ability to identify and assess opportunities and marketplace threats.

Joe and his teams developed their strategy and tactics to capitalize on opportunities and combat threats with all three stakeholders represented.

Another important concept of a high-performance team for Joe was the ability of the team to focus on the business result, then work backwards toward a comprehensive solution that includes customers, people, and stakeholders. A complete solution included all three constituents as well as the approach and the process.

Balance is also important as a leader as you steer the ship through difficult seas. People and organizations do not handle large shifts in vision and philosophy. During difficult times a steady balanced leader can instill confidence in his people, organization, and stakeholders.

A vision and strategy that represents all three constituents from the start is a balanced approach and one that will work through calm and rough seas. At some point all three constituents will need your attention. Do it as part of your approach and not because internal or external pressures force you to do it. Once that happens you risk losing your credibility.

One of the stories Joe likes to tell that highlights this thought goes like this:

The CEO of a large company felt it was time for a visit to the plant. Although this was out of character for him he was getting pressure from shareholders as well as his people. He wanted to demonstrate his decision-making ability and wanted to make an impression with his people. He thought if he could take on some issues and show he was authoritative he would gain their respect even though this was clearly out of character for him.

On the tour of the facility, the CEO noticed a guy leaning on a wall in the room he was entering for a town hall meeting. The room was full of workers and he wanted to let them know he meant business.

He walked up to the guy leaning against the wall and with the crowd watching and listening, asked, "How much do you make in a week?"

A little surprised, the young man looked at him and replied "$400 a week. Why?"

The CEO took out his wallet and then handed the guy $1,600 in cash and screamed, "Here is four weeks' pay. Now get out of here and don't come back!"

Feeling pretty good about himself that he had made a statement, the CEO looked around the room and with great confidence and bravado asked, "Does anyone want to tell me what that goof-ball did here?"

From across the room came a voice: " Yeah. He is the pizza delivery guy!"

In this story the CEO is out of balance, out of character, and out of place. All situations he created. He played roulette with his credibility and reputation and lost.

Our leader lost touch with who he was, what he stood for, and what he wouldn't compromise and conceded to the pressures he was feeling, real or perceived. A balanced leader takes inventory of their own strengths and weaknesses, assesses the situation, understands their people, and seeks guidance under the proper circumstances.

Take care of how and to whom you communicate, and don't get caught up in your position. Be true to yourself so in turn you can be true to your people.

When it comes to providing leadership and setting expectations, commit to yourself and your people to move in one direction.

Unlike the CEO in the story, it is important to communicate often and well to ensure your people understand and embrace change. It's one of the easiest things you can do. It reflects positively on you. Soon you'll find you are inspiring a deep-rooted commitment among all of your people where they model the right values and principles of Balanced Leadership.

The goal is to create a vision centered on the customer and supported by your people and stakeholders. This includes communicating with, educating, and training your people; aligning performance goals; and focusing on accountability. What it does not include is the leader being unbalanced or out of character to support their needs.

A confident, balanced leader must understand that the goals will be achieved through disciplined people, disciplined thought, and disciplined action.

You may have to change your speed and approach but the vision, strategy, mission, and values will not change and are reinforced and applied quicker and more deeply by the resolve of the leader.

As the leader you must set the standards for what "good looks like" and replicate it in everything you do. Clearly in our story this was not done by the CEO because he lost sight of who he was and what he stood for.

As leaders, we must always be constructively dissatisfied—continuously improving our business processes, improving our own skills, and developing our people.

Bottom line: *Maintain your balance.*

THE LESSON:
BALANCE AND ALIGNMENT ARE ESSENTIAL.

» A leader's vision and strategy must align with the organization's vision and strategy.

» The leader must take into consideration the needs and opportunities of associates, customers, and investors. Balanced leaders view their business through the lens of these key constituents.

» Stay true to yourself, your values, and your principles.

CHAPTER 9
THINK LIKE A WHO?

Think like a customer. It's pretty straightforward. But what does it really mean? How did Joe breathe life into this concept for his customers to experience and his people to understand? He knew it was essential to create a brand identity from a customer perspective and get his team to execute the organization's customer strategy. He started to write:

- Put yourselves in your customers' shoes. View things from their perspective.
- Look for ways to help. Don't ignore problems. Acknowledge the customer.
- Customers should be better off because of their interaction with you. Treat them well.
- Serve your customers with energy, creativity, and enthusiasm for their business.

Joe thought this was a good list but maybe it started sooner than this with a few pointed questions, the most important being *Who is your customer?* This seemed like a very simple question that Joe had learned can lead to hours of discussion. At times it may be the question that is the most difficult to get a consensus on, but it needs to be answered before building a customer strategy.

Why is this question so difficult? Joe thought of some of the most engaging conversations he had had over his career, both inside his organization and with customers themselves.

He thought of a supply-chain solution he had worked on in the healthcare space. As the solution was being developed in concert with the customer, the question was asked, *Who is the customer?* Some in the group responded, "the patient." Others responded, "the heath care provider." Or "the vendor network." And still others, "the hospital, clinics, and pharmaceutical company."

At times all may be right, but in this particular solution and for this strategy, the question had to be answered before they could move forward. Who is the customer? Once you establish this critical point, he reasoned, then you can establish some very important next steps in the process:

- What are you solving for?
- What won't you compromise?
- What are your boundaries?
- What keeps the customer awake at night?
- What are the key metrics that you will hold yourself accountable to?
- What does good look like?

There are many other examples, but this is a fundamental question that must be answered to ensure everyone is in sync. Joe always allowed the most time in a strategy kickoff meeting to address this question. He was never disappointed in the dialogue and believed it drove the group to think more creatively.

This simple but powerful exercise helps set the proper expectations for all involved. Expectations are an important part of a solution. Actual results compared to expectations, real or perceived, are an area that drives success, and often disappointment.

Joe is in the zone and just as he is about to begin his next thought he hears the "DING" across the cabin. "Folks, this is your captain speaking. It looks like there is some turbulence ahead and I am going to turn on the seat belt sign. Flight attendants please return to your seats and as soon as it smooths out, I will turn off the seat belt sign, which will be your indication that it is safe to move about the cabin and at that point we will continue our service. I do not expect it to be long. Thank you for your patience."

Captain Aero is Joe's kind of professional. He thinks ahead, anticipates problems, and communicates timely and effectively. But before he can get too caught up in accolades, he remembers Nonna. He looks over and, thankfully, she is still fast asleep. Joe could only hope that the turbulence would not be enough to wake her.

Taking inventory and finding that all is good, with a tug on his seat belt he gets back into the zone.

Setting expectations is a critical component of success, whether it is for yourself as a leader, your area of responsibility, or the services you provide as part of your brand promise. When we hit the mark and the results are good we all bask in the glory of success.

Unfortunately, mistakes happen and delays occur and sometimes we get ahead of ourselves and overcommit and underdeliver when the original commitment was a good expectation. We will now be judged by the customer with a new set of standards and expectations. The rose-colored glasses come off and we will now be viewed by the customer through the lens of a service disconnect or disappointment.

We now have the opportunity to fix the broken promise or compound it when we set a new expectation and then disappoint the customer again. We double down and compound it with a poor explanation of the service disconnect, which ironically we created.

There are many different types of examples that can be cited and used as case studies. To a frequent flier none is more profound than the story Joe loves to tell about flight expectations.

The story goes like this: As a flier you are prepared for a certain flight time as communicated to you when you booked your flight. As an example, Joe is prepared for a four hour and 45 minute wheels up to touchdown flight time and it is reaffirmed by the pilot in the greeting announcements. Your plans and expectation are based on this and that is what you are prepared for. All of your schedules are based on this flight time, which was given in advance and again reassured by the pilot.

As is customary at about the halfway point through the flight the pilot gets on the PA and gives everyone an update. The pilot can tell the passengers one of three things: we are early, we are on time, or we will be late. All three will set actions and expectations in motion from do nothing to feeling excitement that we are early or disappointment that we are late.

Remember, the pilot is about to reset expectations. What will he do in our example? In our example he tells the passengers they are making good time, and they have caught a tailwind and are now scheduled to arrive at their destination 20 minutes early. Good news, right?

He has changed the expectation and the customers are now rearranging their schedules and excited about getting in 20 minutes early. A new standard has been set, and from this point forward anything less than the additional 20 minutes early would be a disappointment. About 20 minutes from the airport in our example, the pilot tells the crew over the loudspeaker to prepare for landing; they have been cleared.

At this point the pilot is looking like a hero as well as the airline. After a smooth landing and prior to arriving at their gate, they stop on the ramp. A concern comes over the faces of the passengers in anticipation of the next announcement.

The pilot addresses the anxious passengers, who are on their cell phones rearranging their schedules. He begins, "As you know we are 20 minutes early, but unfortunately our gate is not available. It should not be too long."

A disappointment runs through the cabin and everyone thinks, *We have been in the air for over four hours; it is not like we showed up unexpectedly.* People are not looking at each other in the tower saying, "Wow. Where did this flight come from? Who knew?" A good situation is now becoming a bad one and an on-time arrival is becoming a disappointment.

After 20 minutes, the plane has not moved from the tarmac when the pilot comes on for an update. He says, "The plane at our gate is ready to push back, but unfortunately there is traffic on the ramp. It should not be more then 5 to 10 minutes before we get to our gate." We all think to ourselves, *This is not the turnpike at rush hour, these are scheduled flights, and any traffic is caused by someone or something. Planes just don't show up unannounced.* At this point a good situation has become a bad situation and is leading to disgruntled customers.

It is all about setting expectations, delivering on the expectations, and when expectations are not met, explaining why in a timely manner.

In our story the pilot's role was to provide information on the flight, but he did not need to set a new expectation. He had flown into this airport many times. There was a greater chance there would be congestion as opposed to the optimistic projection of getting to the gate early. He could have told the passengers they were making good time and were scheduled for an on-time arrival. Then, he would thank them for flying with him and state that they'd hear back from him as they began their initial approach. It would have been short and simple and kept people excited about being on time. If they are early, they are delighted; if they are on time, they are happy; and if they are slightly late, they chalk it up to Newark.

When you *think like a customer* you understand that the biggest differentiator between you and your competitors is the consistent superior customer experience you provide. During every customer interaction your reputation is on the line.

THE LESSON:
SET CLEAR EXPECTATIONS AND MAINTAIN
THEM TO AVOID UNNECESSARY CONFUSION
AND DISAPPOINTMENT.

» Thinking like a customer is the act of understanding the customer—their requirements and expectations.

» Your goal is to meet and exceed their requirements and expectations. If you change expectations, do so strategically and with deliberate processes that are well communicated and understood.

» It means shifting the focus from your agenda to the customer's agenda. It means adjusting to fit your customers' needs and wants rather than your wants and needs.

CHAPTER 10

EVERYTHING IS FINE

Joe looked at his watch and realized they were more than halfway home. He thought about seeing Adrianne and getting caught up on the week's activities over dinner. They were empty nesters and were going out to dinner more now than when all the kids were home.

The routine was always the same: Although Joe professed to be "Gumby" (his term for being Mr. Flexible), the conversation always started with him asking, "Where would you like to go, Hon?" Adrianne would reply a certain restaurant. Joe would frown and then ask, "Is that really where you want to go?"

Her response would be, "Yes, that is why I suggested it, but it doesn't sound like you want to go there so you pick a place."

Joe would oblige and then pick his favorite Italian restaurant. It was amazing, no matter where they lived, he would find that comfortable stop that became his *favorite location*. Chicago, Syracuse, Iowa, to name a few, all had their signature restaurants for Joe.

Giovanni's was the current location, off the beaten path but with great food and old-school atmosphere. Besides being the staple for Friday pizza night, the family was using them for other events. Until recently, Giovanni's was never crowded and had an intimate atmosphere. As they would leave after a great meal, Joe would turn to Adrianne and wonder how they made ends meet—it was never crowded. He thought, the secret would get out and then the crowds, but if it did he hoped it wouldn't be Friday night at 6:00.

As he thought about his response to dinner he realized he might shock her with his response. Tonight might be different.

As he sat on the plane, he thought about his last two experiences at the restaurant and both were not good. Both times the wait for their food was extremely long and Joe was not happy with how they had handled the situation. The secret was out.

The staff realized after much complaining from the customers that the wait was very long and had started to become a pattern of service the last few Friday nights. The manager sent the staff around to talk to all the customers and explain that the restaurant was becoming a very crowded and popular place. The kitchen was backed up.

Joe thought, *Isn't this what they had hoped for when they opened their business? How has their problem become my problem?*

As Joe was paying the bill the cashier asked him, "How was everything?" Joe used the proverbial killer word in the customer service vocabulary. He responded that everything was "Fine."

"Fine" is commonly used by people who are not happy but do not want to discuss it and are ready to move on. Joe was one of those individuals. He responded politely "fine" and had no intention of going back. The restaurant asked a question they felt obligated to ask, accepted an answer they know could not be correct after all of the complaints they received that night, and they lost a customer and revenue they might never see again. The owner may preach customer service, the staff may be polite, and the food may be good, but no one sat at the table and viewed the dinner through the eyes of the customer.

That night after the restaurant was closed, the owner may have asked the staff, "How did it go tonight? How were your customers?" No doubt their answer to him was, "FINE." To Joe, the sad part of this story is that they easily could have turned a bad situation into a great situation.

When you think like a customer, the dialogue could go something like this: "We are sorry for the delay, but thanks for your patience and business. We realize the last few weeks we have been busy and it has resulted in longer than expected delays in getting your meals. We are addressing the situation and we are committed to getting it fixed. Thank you again for your patience and please join us again and have a dessert on us."

Joe would be all over the cannoli and espresso, and would absolutely give them another chance. Instead, Joe will have to find a new favorite restaurant before Adrianne beats him to it.

Thinking like a customer is more than a slogan. Thinking like a customer is your way of doing business; it is the approach you won't compromise.

It is the acceptance that the biggest differentiator between you and your competitors is the superior customer experience you provide. During every customer interaction your reputation is on the line.

Joe had come to learn and believe that when you truly think like a customer, your view is from their perspective. You look at things differently—through their eyes. For example, you now begin to gather and analyze customer data to discover business opportunities that you may have never seen before. You look to continuously improve your customer's value and cement customer retention. You begin to develop a competitive advantage that helps you both to grow. Finally, when you think like a customer, you begin to identify high potential business opportunities and create innovative products and services that allow you and your customer to be first to market.

THE LESSON:
WHEN YOUR PROBLEMS BECOME
THE CUSTOMERS' PROBLEM THEY LEAVE.
A SERVICE DISRUPTION IS NOT FINE.

- » Customer-focused companies and businesses consistently outperform the competition.

- » Customers have enough of their own problems; they do not need yours.

- » Balanced leaders teach their team to think like a customer and be solution providers.

- » Consistently demonstrate to customers you are attuned to their needs and are operating in their best interest. Customers know what they want but may not always explain it in a manner that is clear to you. Therefore, it is important that effective listening skills are utilized. If you do not understand a request, ask clear, positively articulated questions until you understand. Do not rush customers; allow them to discuss what they need at their own pace. Once customers have expressed their needs, confirm your understanding with them to ensure communication is clear.

CHAPTER 11
FEEL LIKE A VALUED INDIVIDUAL

As Joe was stretching and beginning his normal restlessness toward the last part of the flight, the person in the aisle seat next to him bumped him on their way to placing their bag back in the overhead bin. He smiled at Joe and before he could apologize Joe looked at him with that, "Been there, done that before" smile that said all was good. Joe could not help but notice that in the overhead bin was a piece of luggage that had flight crew tags on it. Looking around, Joe did not see anyone dressed as an employee of this or any airline.

It prompted Joe to think about his walks around the operations and how he could never be the "Undercover Boss." Joe was not critical of the show or its premise, but felt his style was more suited to the TV show *Cheers*.

Joe took great pride in the fact he was the kind of leader that everyone knew his name. He often took the time to reflect on the values and principles of the company and felt that this alignment was key to building a strong company culture. This created the atmosphere where people felt they were valued. He often asked himself, *What do I do as a leader to create the environment where all the people in my care and responsibility feel like they are a valued?*

Leadership is all about setting the direction and establishing the necessary culture to succeed. As valued individuals, could his people answer these questions?

- Am I part of the solution, not part of the problem?
- My thoughts and ideas matter. Can I be a thought leader?
- Do I build relationships with peers, customers, and the entire team?
- Do I accept safety and integrity as core values?
- Does my authority equal my responsibility?
- Do I learn everything I can about my job, then do I learn some more?

As leaders, we have a major influence on the performance and behavior of our people. We can leverage the tools of the various functions within an organization, which can help to drive efficiencies and connect people with information and processes. Joe was a firm believer that you must continue this emphasis on learning and leadership, as well as communicating with your associates about the goals and performance as a way of life and not the flavor of the day. The more employees understand what's expected of them and where the organization is headed, the better able they are to align themselves and work efficiently to accomplish goals.

Joe's mind drifted to a conversation he had with his dad. *Star Trek* was all the rage when Joe was growing up and early on Joe watched *Star Trek* religiously.

A few months into the show his dad asked, "I notice you have stopped watching *Star Trek*. What's going on?"

Joe responded, "I do not trust or like a show that each week professes as its mission, 'to boldly go where no man has gone before' and each week they find someone."

Joe was all about trust and doing what you said you were going to do. Joe always kept the *Star Trek* experience as his double check: what did we say we were going to do and did we do it?

Joe believed he was the type of person and leader that focused on values. Joe also felt there was a significant point in the evolution of a leader where intrinsic statements must be formalized and understood, so everyone in the organization conducts themselves from the same platform and it started with him.

For Joe it was something as simple but powerful as trying to never refer to his people as being under his supervision but rather in his care.

As Joe matured and grew as a leader, he set his leadership style and vision to be in sync with the company's culture and direction. To provide the ability for the people in his care to feel like valued individuals, they must work in an environment where they felt valued, where their work mattered. Simply put, if they did not come to work someone would notice and care.

Joe often heard the term "employer of choice." Joe asked himself when he first heard it, what does it mean to be an employer of choice? He believed if he understood what the term meant, if it supported his beliefs that people were his most important asset, and it created an environment where people felt valued, then he was all in for creating an employer of choice environment in his operation.

There are many factors that make a company desirable to work for, he thought: *compensation programs, health and welfare plans, work-life balance, performance and recognition programs, along with career development opportunities are the most obvious and are important.*

What makes a job more than a job and a company more than average, he reasoned, is when you feel like a valued individual—a member of the family. Your work matters and you can make a difference. Joe hoped that the people in his care always felt this way. Joe loved being a part of a family and he hoped to create that same feeling at work.

He would often say that when your people are in that place where they feel valued, it's often because of alignment. They are in alignment with the company's values. They believe in the mission and vision. Your people understand the value proposition that differentiates their company from the next. When all these factors coexist, employee satisfaction increases. When employees are engaged to this degree, they are focused on what matters most—customer service.

As Joe was stretching he noticed that the woman in the aisle seat a few rows up was unwrapping some Hershey chocolate. Hershey is an iconic brand founded in 1894 by Milton S. Hershey in Hershey, Pennsylvania. The Hershey Company story is a great American story and Joe's version is a great American story with a Scafone twist. It has a special place with Joe.

His version added the belief that if you are going to build a solid business relationship with your customers, it can only happen when your customers start trusting you and they value your advice. This only happens when your view is centered on the customer rather than yourself or your company. You add a customer's view to the story line.

He often would say that as a leader and a person you have an "aha" moment that will last with you forever and becomes that significant moment that creates a change in you. The Hershey story was a significant "aha" moment for Joe.

When Joe was a child, he and his family had the opportunity to visit the Hershey Chocolate Factory in Hershey, Pennsylvania. It was amazing to see all that chocolate up close, his taste buds ablaze.

All Joe could think of was the chocolate and how cool it was to see it made. In those days you actually toured the factory. You saw the chocolate being made as if the factory was under glass. You saw the workers as they went about their responsibilities with great pride and joy as if no one but them was in the factory. What also left an impression on Joe after all these years was touring the factory and seeing the chocolate being made by hardworking local people from beginning to end.

Years later, as Joe was touring his own operation, he realized the confidence the Hershey organization must have had in their people as literally thousands of people walked through their factory each day while they made their famous chocolate bars. Joe wondered, *Can a customer walk through my operation unannounced and still be impressed with my organization?*

Joe asked himself, *Do I run a Hershey factory? Can my customers walk through my operations anytime and would they be proud of what they saw?* From that day, Joe challenged himself and his staff to inspire those in their care to be as confident in their people and operations as Hershey is in theirs. If they could do so, their customers would enjoy the same experience in one of their facilities—confident and excited to see their products are in our hands. As a leader, regardless of your area of responsibility, you have your own "Hershey factory." You need to make sure your customers would be equally proud of what they see in your facilities, people, and solutions.

From that significant event forward, Joe combined that vision and the empowerment of his people, who felt valued in everything they did. He wanted growth by having the right processes, such as those that ensure safety; the appropriate use of assets like fleet and facilities; specific operational excellence measures; and a committed team of talented people who believed that they were the best, brightest, most informed, and best educated in the industry.

To Joe these are the key ingredients needed to meet and exceed customers' needs and expectations and truly demonstrate the strength of your brand. In Joe's view, you think like a customer because you feel like a valued individual. His people needed to be a catalyst for change; to understand, accept, and live the company's vision and mission; and to emulate the company values in all they do.

Joe reasoned that innovation and creativity created opportunity, but a winning team that is committed to building an unbeatable brand is what created demand and growth. As a valued individual, excellence becomes more than competence; you are now striving for the highest possible results because you know that your work matters. You engage with customers and work with each other, knowing that the work you do is a self-portrait. You are more motivated by *doing the "right thing" rather than "things right."* Ultimately, valued individuals understand that working together works for Hershey factories everywhere.

THE LESSON:

VALUE THOSE ON YOUR TEAM WHO WORK
TIRELESSLY TO CREATE "AHA" MOMENTS
FOR YOUR BRAND.

» Effective leaders create a culture of excellence that manifests itself in the daily actions of their associates and ultimately defines your brand. They are your "value added."

» Building a business relationship is the same as building a personal relationship.

» The quality of the relationship is directly proportional to your efforts to build. When you feel like a valued individual you are more likely to put in the time and effort to build these relationships.

» Creating a strong culture is critical to a company's long-term success and growth. It should be the desire of the senior leadership team to create the best, brightest, most informed and best-educated people in the industry.

CHAPTER 12

YOUR CANDY STORE

Joe thought about the concept of acting like an owner. What were the traits of an owner? How should he act if he was the company's owner? Joe began to write down what he viewed as essential ownership traits:

- Owners have the vision to look ahead to create a compelling sense of purpose and validity. Know and go to where the puck is going.
- Walk the talk.
- Be an effective communicator. Have clarity, credibility, and persuasiveness with all constituents.
- Use sound judgment and make thoughtful decisions.
- Be results oriented. Drive the process to achieve breakthrough performance.

- Never compromise integrity and ethics. (Remember, it's what you do when no one is watching that counts.)
- Get the market pulse in all segments by thinking like a customer; then create brand loyalty by delighting customers.
- Own the problem, not just the results.

Joe thought he had compiled a comprehensive list and they were still not on the ground. His last flight as a business professional was flying by. Did he miss the announcement that said we are in our initial decent, which was the 20-minute-out notification? He looked around and everyone was busy doing their thing. Then he remembered, as part of the in-flight service, the flight tracker gives you time to destination; he would check that.

According to the flight tracker there was an hour left in the flight. This was validated by the announcement that the flight attendants would be coming through the cabin for their final beverage service before landing. Okay. We are in sync.

He thought back to his list and his way of always thinking of things in simple terms that people could see, touch, and understand. Maybe this was because Joe never viewed himself as the smartest man in the room.

He would often say that when one train leaves New York and another leaves California he is not the person who could tell you when the trains would meet in the middle; that was better left for the smarter people. But when the passengers got off the train they would be happy, motivated, focused people and they would know the purpose of the trip.

This ability to understand that the greatest thing he didn't know was what he didn't know allowed him to be open to collaboration. Joe always believed you viewed solutions from their widest consequences.

If you could understand and anticipate these consequences, you then had the opportunity to limit the number of surprises along the way. Joe knew that there would always be unintended consequences that he and his team would need to navigate through. But if you could limit them and try to anticipate them, you gave yourself the best chance for success.

Many times the surprises were loose lug nuts that developed along the way. Joe wanted to make sure they were tightened as they happened. To breathe life into this ownership concept Joe would take his people through a series of questions designed to understand the solution, view it from its widest consequences, and determine if it was a balanced approach. As the group or a person approached the final decision, Joe would ask the most important question last: "If this was your candy store would you make this decision?"

Joe wanted his people, especially those presenting the solution, to view the solution through the eyes of an owner. The question was simple and direct: if this was your candy store or Hershey factory would you do this? If new associates were present, he would ask them to imagine if they owned their own candy store. As owners, they'd know how much their candy supply costs and who supplied the candy at the best rates. They would develop relationships with those suppliers and communicate well with them.

They would provide better service than the candy shop down the street, knowing their job is to delight those who do business with their store so they would return again and again, for more and more candy. As the store owner, they would know when to reward employees, as well as when to make hard decisions when your workers aren't being safe.

As an owner, they would know how much was needed to sell, to whom, and how often to make a profit. After a hard day's work, what was in the cash register would be paid to their people and vendors, and what was left, if anything, is what you take home to your family. This is a true profit-and-loss perspective and the ultimate in thinking like an owner.

Joe was not looking to discourage his people, but he wanted to make sure they took ownership for the problem as well as the solution. As an owner in your part of your business, what is the expectation you have for your products and services, and how committed are you to the results?

As an owner, you also know that you are not allowed to silently sanction bad behavior. If in the candy store some employees saw a coworker taking candy home every day for their family, they might look the other way. They might rationalize that they do not need or want to get involved; some might say, "It is not my candy, it is not my store." However, those who act like an owner would address the situation promptly. They are taking money out of the cash register before the bills and employees are paid and potentially putting your family in jeopardy.

There are many instances where a leader sees a situation that must be addressed but looks the other way or ignores it. This is unacceptable behavior for a leader. As a leader you cannot silently sanction bad behavior. This responsibility to address issues as you see them is one of the biggest reasons that many leaders do not manage by walking around because they recognize they have ZERO chance of seeing bad behaviors they would have to address if they never leave their office.

Joe accepts the responsibility and manages by walking around. One of his peers, Claude Rains, is a "see no evil" manager who never leaves his office. Joe has often pointed out to Claude that this is a short-sighted and dangerous view of his leadership responsibilities. Joe would explain to Claude that if you marginalize and denigrate compliance, ethical behavior, legal and operational issues, you are only putting off today what you will have to address tomorrow in a bigger way. These are lug nuts that cause major accidents when they are not tightened and addressed. The consequences for an owner not tightening the lug nuts may result in a loss of their business, reputation, or worse.

Joe also believed that the view from an ownership perspective also helped to achieve the greatest balance. Not only did Joe walk the talk, he was an avid communicator, believing it should result in a culture of trust, empowerment, and inclusion.

As a balanced leader, he felt trust was essential even if there wasn't always agreement in decisions. We all have disagreements with people we care about, but in the end we trust them. Trust is not a popularity contest but simply doing what you said you would do. When we can disagree without being disagreeable, that is trust. He also realized there are some who will choose to sit on the sidelines and offer many suggestions with no real commitment to fix or change anything. Owners cannot afford to sit on the sidelines. Owners have to be in it to win it.

Openness and trust are slow to rise and quick to fall. As Joe walked around his operations with a view as an owner he would often ask himself, who has the best chance of succeeding, of achieving and sustaining operational excellence? The answer was always work groups with the highest level of trust.

He would then ask himself one more question. How does a work group's level of trust affect the customer? Trust leads to employee loyalty and, ultimately, customer satisfaction. The customers simply don't care about our internal grievances.

As an owner, what would you want for your business? You would certainly want repeat business. Repeat business, or customer loyalty, gives us the opportunity to build relationships with customers and anticipate what value-added services they may need now and into the future.

Owners also understand the value of employee retention and customer retention because it is a lot more expensive to replace a lost customer than to retain a loyal one. Owners understand the value of doing things right the first time. The cost of rework is sometimes greater than the original cost.

Acting like an owner may be the most difficult balancing act in the balanced leadership playbook. So much of Joe's foundation and views were formed in his childhood by his parents, family, school, and in particular his father. In his adult life he was fortunate to work with and be around some excellent business professionals as well as great family and friends. His greatest influence in his adult life was his wife, Adrianne.

To Joe, Adrianne was the greatest example of ownership and balance. Raising four children through the many moves across the country was the ultimate test of parenting, patience, and commitment. Joe's ultimate lesson on ownership and balance came from her.

One Friday night Joe and Adrianne had been invited to dinner with a couple they had met in church. They had three children of their own. One day, they asked how the children handled the moves at their different ages and school grades. Jokingly the couple asked, "Do you have a favorite child through all of this?"

Adrianne smiled and said, "Each of them believes they are the favorite, because I believe that they each got what they needed when they needed it. When each of them was the focus of attention it was because that is what they needed at that time."

Joe never forgot that explanation. She was the glue that held the family together and had a wonderful instinct about parenting. She was the balanced parent, who listened to the children and made them feel like they were the most important person with her undivided attention when they needed it but acted like a mom. From that day forward Joe understood what acting like an owner meant. Customers, people, and stakeholders got what they needed—his time, attention, focus, and commitment—when they needed it.

THE LESSON:

OWNERS ALWAYS STRIVE TO FIND THE BETTER WAY; THE BEST WAY IS WHEN IT INCLUDES YOUR CUSTOMERS AND YOUR PEOPLE.

» Understand the value of doing things right the first time.

» A leader cannot silently sanction bad behavior or ignore a problem.

» Openness and trust are slow to rise and quick to fall.

» Balanced leaders build and maintain trust, which leads to employee loyalty and, ultimately, customer satisfaction.

CHAPTER 13
BUILDING CATHEDRALS

It was time for their descent into Newark's Liberty International Airport. Joe's routine was orderly and everything had its place in his briefcase. One of the last things Joe packed up was his old friend— his desk planner and calendar. Although he understood and embraced technology, there was no substitute for his paper calendar filled with dates and handwritten notes. Joe had one for every year going back over 20 years. In the back of the calendar was a notes and a diary section that Joe penned during the year with thoughts, visions, problems, and solutions.

After stowing his belongings Joe looks at his watch. He thinks, *This flight has literally flown by,* as his head was full of great memories and stories. Nonna is starting to wake from a very relaxing sleep. Just as she is ready to ask Joe a question, Captain Antonio makes his announcement: "Ladies and gentleman, as we start our descent, please make sure your seat backs and tray tables are in their full upright and locked position. Make sure your seat belt is securely fastened and all carry-on luggage is stowed underneath the seat in front of you or in the overhead bins. Thank you for flying with us and I will see you on the ground."

"You and Antonio did well for yourselves. Your mothers must be proud," exclaimed Nonna. Joe smiled. No matter how much you might think of your career or accomplishments, rest assured your mother, grandmother, and family was there to assure you of your extraordinary qualities and talent and to keep you grounded. You can always count on your family!

She then asked Joe, "Do you think Antonio had something to eat?"

Joe assured her that they had brought him something to eat. This trip with Nonna gave Joe a chance to think and reflect on a wonderful career and a great family. Growing up Italian was unique and Joe thought about some of those fun moments.

In an Italian family, when your friends came over they were always asked if they wanted something to eat. You have multiple cousins named Maria, Christina, Vinny, or Michael, and at least one Uncle Tony. You can expect to repeat and spell out your last name whenever anyone hears it for the first time and often you get asked, "What's your real name?" Of course, especially being from Jersey, you had to explain to people that the show *Jersey Shore* was not an accurate portrayal of Italian Americans.

You also realize some of the things you took for granted may not have been the norm. Not everyone eats fish on Christmas Eve; you may be the only people who call good family friends aunt and uncle.

Just before the wheels hit the ground, Nonna grabbed Joe's arm and held it tight. Nothing was said but a reassuring hold was all she needed. Once the plane was safely on the ground, Nonna made the sign of the cross and quietly thanked all the saints she had been talking to on the descent. The plane arrived at the gate. Antonio had delighted his customers and exceeded their expectations with his and his team's performance.

As he unfastened his seatbelt Joe thought, *It wasn't about being Italian, or Catholic. It wasn't about your religious affiliation, country of origin or sexual preference. It was about embracing who you are, what you stand for, and what you won't compromise.*

For Joe it was always about leaving the place a little better than he found it.

Joe offered to walk Nonna to the baggage carousel even though he had only taken a carry-on with him.

"Who is picking you up?" he asked. She explained it was her son Giorgio, but you could call him George. "He is my second of four," she replied. "Why don't I tell you about him? He is a wonderful boy, but all of my children are beautiful kids."

Joe smiled to himself. Nonna is a balanced mom and grandmother who understands that all her children are individuals within the family unit. No one is more important than the rest and each get what they need when they need it.

Nonna continued, "He is an excellent craftsman, a highly skilled machinist. He has worked for the same company for over 35 years."

"It sounds like he has done very well for himself."

With a proud smile Nonna declares, "He would give you the shirt off his back. He has done well for himself and his family; I am very proud of him."

Joe and Nonna were talking about her other children as they approached the carousel. Anthony was number three, a good son who was good as gold and very generous. She proudly told Joe, everyone loves him.

The youngest was Mary. She prayed to Mary for a girl after three boys and her thanks was naming her only daughter after her. Her description was simple but moving and powerful. She was the most inspirational person she knew.

As they reach the carousel, she waves to George to get his attention as he is gathering up her luggage.

"You haven't told me about your oldest," he says.

"My oldest is Rocco," she replies. "He is a hardworking business-man who is just finishing a long career with a great company. He started with the company during college."

George comes over to greet her with a warm smile and a hug. She introduces Joe to her son. Joe and Giorgio exchange pleasantries, he thanks Joe for looking after his mother, and Joe thanks Nonna for a great trip. She gives him a big hug, tells him to say hello to the family and get home safely. As she starts to walk away, she stops, turns to Joe with a smile and tells him, "You know, you are a like my oldest son." With that she walks away.

Joe thinks to himself as he watches Nonna walk away, *Leadership is a concept that is not reserved for, and only applies to, certain people in business, government, civic organizations, or a family. The reality is no matter our age, gender, occupation, educational level, or position in life, each of us touches and influences other lives. Through this extension we are all leaders to someone at some time. It can be a person under our supervision or care, a spouse we honor and live with, or a child we nurture, a student we teach, or a player we coach. It could be as simple as a member of our church or religious affiliation, club, league, or association, but it is usually identified by the fact we have made a positive difference through our actions and examples.*

Those with this sense of responsibility are constantly in pursuit of knowl-edge about how to be a good leader, mentor, and person and how we can im-prove our skills. We take great pride in the books we have read and where they sit on the best-seller list. But sometimes these lessons and learning experiences come from the people right in front of us, the people in our care and supervision, the people we engage with every day or someone next to us on a plane.

Many of these lessons come from your friends and family and are free if you choose to accept them. This is the ultimate friends and family discount. And sometimes it is as simple as a story we learned as children or read to our children as parents or grandparents.

Joe thinks about how these interactions, whether at home, in school, on the playground, in outside organizations, with your family, or on the shop floor, and how by their nature they help to develop emotional intelligence, creativity, and personal growth. These experiences can nurture growth and develop a person's personality and social skills. These are all skills we aspire to and are trying to develop as leaders. These experiences and the interactions with mentors, role models, family members, and the disappointments of life allow us the opportunity to respond and develop our own opinions about topics but within the guidelines of right and wrong and moral and ethical behavior.

Leaders must develop emotional intelligence along with their educational intelligence and business acumen. Sometimes a simple interaction with a sincere honest person can help you see the bigger picture, promote moral and ethical behavior, and maybe just help you not take yourself so seriously that you lose sight of the fact that it is not always about you.

Leaders must set the tone from the top like my dad, Nonna, and Adrianne. Although they may not realize it, they had a clearly defined mission and a unified sense of purpose, helping the family to have a sense of clarity and values.

The leader must ensure that everyone is working together and everyone checks their agenda at the door. Put another way, everyone must understand the destination and how we are getting there and their roles in getting us there. The leader must articulate the vision for the organization, the team, and/or the family.

Nonna is a good person, with honesty of purpose and a clear vision of what she wants for her family. Sometimes the greatest lessons are right in front of you. Maybe Nonna was the exclamation point on a wonderful career, a gift from my dad for the ride home.

It is all in the way you choose to see things:

Three people were laboring in a field of boulders and large stones. Sweat ran from their foreheads as they swung their heavy picks again and again. A curious passerby approached them and asked each what they were doing.

The first person answered in a stern and abrupt voice, "Can't you see? I am breaking rocks!" The second person replied in a matter-of-fact way, "Can't you see? I am earning my salary!" The third person smiled—their eyes gleaming with enthusiasm—and proclaimed, "Can't you see? I am helping to build a Cathedral!"

There is no doubt that Nonna thinks like the third person in this story. Leadership, parenting, and mentoring are not passive duties; they are active responsibilities. All of us make the choice of our leadership style and how we inspire people.

You will not be judged by the number of degrees on your wall, the number of promotions that you receive, or the accolades you receive from friends and groups. Rather it will come from the answer to the question: Are the people and places that you have touched better because of their interactions with you? Did you build a cathedral or did you break down your people into tiny rocks?

These are the questions you will have to answer in the quiet of your own heart and conscience.

Joe thought, *I have had many good people work with and for me and I believe that they were positively impacted because of our time together.* That he thought was the exclamation point on a wonderful career filled with great memories and people.

As Joe left the airport to meet Adrianne, he thought about his next journey—retirement. As he moves along and through the good and bad periods on his next journey, Joe always wanted to keep these thoughts from his childhood, family, and career in perspective. Nonna, like his dad in his childhood and Adrianne in his adult life, was that voice of reason and compassion that made it all work. He thought: *Don't let your highs get too high or your lows get too low; tighten the lug nuts, and leave everything you touch better than you found it.*

THE LESSON:

LEADERSHIP IS AN ACTIVE RESPONSIBILITY,
NOT A PASSIVE DUTY.

» Every person leads another at some point. Continuous learning and sharing helps develop emotional and educational intelligence and business acumen.

» You should have a developmental strategy that you can implement with your team. If people development is important to you then it becomes important to them.

CHAPTER 14
THE EPIPHANY

A few weeks had gone by and Joe was in his home office organizing his things and reminiscing as he went through the boxes of writings and memories. He called it the library of Joe. Adrianne called it *his stuff*. This stuff was becoming a third person and he knew he needed to get on it and it needed to find its place.

Two of the last things Joe unpacked were his old friends—his desk planners and calendars. He looked forward to going through his handwritten notes, his walk down memory lane. These calendars and their notes became the heart and soul of Joe the business leader (as well as his playbook).

Joe had kept them all and they provided an insight into his thoughts, visions, problems, and solutions.

As he thumbed through one of the oldest ones, he came across his notes on Balanced Leadership. Joe was often asked when the Balanced Leadership approach started or how it became his game plan for success.

When asked when it started he could never answer exactly, but had a good idea, but now his calendar with dates and time could answer that question. How it evolved and became his hallmark strategy and game plan came from his growth, experiences, and evolution as a leader.

As Joe was evolving into a performance-driven leader he was connected by the principles of Balanced Leadership. This is where you

- think like a customer by approaching each challenge as a true solutions provider;
- feel like a valued individual by knowing your work matters and you are part of the solution, not part of the problem, and you will never compromise on safety and integrity;
- act like an owner by understanding the business and your role in what leads to success.

Believing that consistency was the mark of a champion, he was convinced that the consistency would come from processes that tied it all together and allowed the balanced leader the ability to replicate the results over time and new people.

He embraced this Balanced Leadership philosophy along with the goals and objectives through walking the talk and his daily actions.

In one early calendar, in the notes section, were his original notes on Balanced Leadership and the beginning of this strategic vision. A little later in another calendar came the lug nut story, which became the tactical view of managing time, priorities, and outcomes. These calendars were gold to Joe, a view into his heart and soul.

As Joe begins to read this early notebook he sits down and grabs his coffee and he takes a ride back in time. The Balanced Leadership epiphany is born at a meeting more than 20 years earlier.

The meeting may have started out the same way—introductions, problem statements, some questions—but it ended in a very different way that in retrospect was profound.

The setting is in a small conference room on a very typical day. The group was trying to solve a persistent service issue. Joe was now in a senior leadership role. His confidence was on the rise; he was growing, developing, and starting to hit his stride as a leader. This is evident by the fact that Joe took a different approach in this meeting: he chose to observe and not participate in their problem-solving session.

The group was proud of their collaboration and believed they had developed a new process, a way to track their progress and results and set new standards of success. The team was prepared for their review, knowing Joe would be positive but constructively critical and would always challenge them to "move beyond the first right answer."

Joe's notes begin with his opening remarks to the group. "I am very proud of your work and your ownership of the problem. Your energy and enthusiasm make me very proud and I have great confidence you will get this fixed. I believe you have worked through the process in a collaborative manner so I trust your approach. I have a few questions before we implement this solution."

He proceeds to ask some questions that for him were out of character and outside the box.

"You have defined your goals and set them at a particular level. Your processes to achieve these goals seem to be in sync. These may be the right goals for us to achieve but I have two question about these goals." In his notes, these two questions were underlined and highlighted in yellow.

"First, where are these goals in relationship to our competition and the benchmarks for success that have been established in the industry? Secondly, if we achieved these goals, would our customers be happy or are we still well below their expectations?"

The room became quiet and no one could offer Joe an answer.

Joe proceeded to talk to the group about internal focus. "These are the elements that we believe are important. We are benchmarking our self against our peers in our company and not against the competition or the industry standards. We have to remember that internal competition is good and it may drive results in a positive manner, but in the end we are in competition with the competition and not each other. Secondly the goals we set should be in sync with the goals of our customers. It is what keeps the customer awake at night that then keeps us awake at night." By setting the goals externally, Joe wrote in his notes, you look at it from the customer's perspective.

This concept later became "Think like a customer."

Joe then asked the group, "Who will execute the plan?" The group responded, "Our people."

He proceeded, "Then this will be an area that will need our attention. How will we communicate the plan to get our people to buy into the vision and the solution we have developed?"

When people understand their roles and responsibilities they become empowered. Joe believed that true empowerment is when people discipline themselves. They understand the mission and the goals and do not want to disappoint you or themselves.

In his notes he began to formulate the view and wrote: "If you value your people, you think of them first in everything you do. They are part of the solution, not part of the problem." This was the beginning of "Feel like a valued individual."

Finally, Joe looked at the group and asked the question, "If this was your candy store, if you owned this company 100%, would you be happy with the solution and outcome?"

This was the question they were waiting to answer. This was the question they expected from Joe. The answer, however, was not what Joe had expected.

Their answer now went like this: "We are proud of our solution and we think it can work, but it is our solution and it potentially may not be a solution that delights our customers and empowers our people. Our process may be right but we have to address our approach. Let us go back and take a view from our customer's perspective and then ask a few of our key people their thoughts on implementation and skills training they may need. We will get back to you after we gather this additional information and adjust our plans."

Joe was very proud of them. He admired their openness to learn and not stop at the first right answer. They were willing to be challenged. He also credits this meeting as having two significant events. It was the epiphany of the Balanced Leadership concept and his subsequent approach to business leadership. It also was the moment that Joe the manager became Joe the leader.

Joe the leader came to the realization that leading is not a staged performance. Training, educating, and developing your people means involving them. Razzle-dazzle, a great use of the English language or speaking skills, does not equal leadership success.

Leaders concentrate on getting information from their people, feeding it back, adding additional information to educate them, and then allowing them to make their choices so that they can practice these leadership skills.

This requires excellent listening and the commitment to talk less and listen more.

Joe continued to refine the Balanced Leadership playbook and it became his signature approach to business. For Joe, the hard work and commitment had to be in the area of listening more and talking less.

He came to realize and understand that you earn the right to ask difficult or sensitive questions by the way you consistently address the issues and model effective leadership with honest and ethical behavior to all you represent.

Open and honest communications and visibility are an important element of trust so he took great care to make sure he was available to his people and visible in his operations.

As you move through difficult periods on your way to success, do the "right thing," take care of your customers, treat others with dignity and respect, and celebrate successes and your reward will be "The Leader of Choice." You will create a place where your people will thank you for not letting them stray or compromise their values and ethics. They will be excited about other ways they can participate in successfully reaching their goals and those of the organization.

THE LESSON:
THERE ARE MANY ROUTES AVAILABLE. DEVELOP YOUR MOST STRATEGIC PATH.

» Spend more time observing and asking questions than telling and preaching to develop an effective vision.

» Successful leaders inspire team members at every level to understand, embrace, emulate, and execute the vision and the strategy.

» True empowerment occurs when people discipline themselves and tighten their own lug nuts.

» We have to remember that internal competition is good and it may drive results in a positive manner, but in the end we are in competition with the competition and not each other.

» Leadership is a commitment that requires excellent listening skills and the commitment to talk less and listen more.

CHAPTER 15
100-DAY PLAN

Joe placed his old friend onto his desk with a smile and with great pride as he thought back to that meeting. He also was very proud of how the concept of Balanced Leadership had become his signature approach, his strategy for success. One of the keys to leadership success is to be known for something; it allows you to separate yourself and it helps to define who you are, what you stand for, and what you won't compromise. It is uniquely you.

Before he could get too excited and caught up in the moment he realizes that the rearranging and moving of piles will not count as a productive day of getting his office organized. He now has a loose lug nut and the important task of organizing the home office may be moving from important to urgent at some point with Adrianne.

Jumping into gear, he begins to clear his desk using the philosophy that a relatively neat and orderly desk should buy him some time.

As he quickly stacks and moves some of his calendars, some papers fall out. He saw that one was his 100-Day Plan that he had put together prior to the start of his last assignment. This practice and document was one of the significant events in his evolution as a leader.

He started this process of writing down his 100-Day Plan many years back. Joe would often say that you cannot put the seat belt on after the airbags go off. He realized that his approach to starting a new assignment was a critical first step. You had to start right to stay right.

Joe believed that when it came to providing leadership and setting expectations, it started with him. What his people learned first about him is what they would retain the longest. The speed of the leader determines the pace of the pack and Joe was determined to set the pace. A good plan and vision gave Joe the ability to start right and set the pace and direction. The plan was written in a memo form to his boss and team, and Joe would take it out often to gauge his progress.

He sat back in his office chair and began to read the memo like a person who was watching their favorite movie or reading their favorite book for the first time.

To: Mike
Fr: Joe
Re: 100-day plan

The key component for the first 100 days and beyond is Balanced Leadership. The three constituents that must be in consideration in all we do in the first 100 days as well as going forward are our Customers, our People, and our Stakeholders. In all we do and in all I do as the leader, my actions must take these three into consideration. This is why Balanced Leadership is so important, because everyone will watch and see and evaluate what they believe I believe is important. In all of our decisions we must have balance. We must

Think like a Customer, Feel like a Valuable Individual, and Act like an Owner. As I craft my first 100 days I will do it with this in mind. I also want to reinforce thru any future communication and visits to facilities that I believe the difference between our competitors and us is our people! The ability and desire for them to be the Best, the Brightest, Most Informed and Best-Educated people in the industry is what separates us from our competitors and is a strategic advantage for us! If they do not believe this at this point, they will over the course of the coming weeks, months, and years. It will start in the first 100 days.

Customers . . . I need to visit our top two or three customers in each business unit. I would like to understand the current service metrics, our service recovery procedures, and the depth and breadth of our relationships and who owns them. I am sure each business unit has its version of operations excellence; I would like to understand it and make sure they are not just activities but activities that lead to successes. I believe we need to move toward our customers, and the industries we serve, as seeing us as a solution-based company, which will help us to be less of a commodity and more of a value-added solution provider. We need to understand this concept, our people need to understand the vision, and we need to execute to this vision. I would also like to understand the revenue streams, what is our opportunity to grow and penetrate in our current customer base.

People . . . Through my visits I would like to understand our safety culture. I would like to begin the process of getting our people to understand that they are a part of a great company and that their business unit is an important part of the "Who We Are" as an enterprise and understand that they are part of a bigger entity. This will be a difficult task and will take a lot longer than 100 days but it has to start somewhere, although slow, but it must start. As I visit, talk, and observe, I will get a sense of our training and the quality of our people. There is no substitute for MBWA, management by walking around. I would like to see how deep our communication goes and how effective it is. This will be important as we begin to start to build a unifying culture. It will help us foster the concept of the best, brightest, most informed and best-educated people in the industry. Does someone own communication? Is it a passion or a task? Does everyone understand the mission, strategy, and priorities?

Ownership . . . Understand each business unit's business plan before I go out and visit their operations and let them tell me their business plan as they understand it. Here is where I usually see big disconnects. What are the important leading indicators? What are we tracking, and what are they tracking and where and why are we disconnected? Will these metrics lead to a successful month and quarter? As we prepare for our customer visits and reviews, the quality of revenue and the DSO (days sales outstanding) piece will be important. I will work with finance and business development to make sure we understand this piece. Do we understand at every level the role we play in driving results for the corporation, our business unit, and what leads to this success? Does each of us own our results and take responsibility for the good, the bad, and the areas that need improvement?

At the end of the first 100 days I would like to be able to answer these questions from my visits, interactions, and communications:

Who are the primary customers in each business unit? This is more than the name of a customer. It is who the customer is, what the opportunities with that customer are. Who is our top churned customer in each business unit and why?

How do we, our leaders, our people prioritize our core values of our customers, our people, and stakeholders?

What are the critical performance metrics that are being tracked in each staff function and business unit, and do they meet the expectations of all three constituents?

What strategic boundaries are we willing to set? What are the things or areas that won't be compromised?

Do we create positive creative tension, or is there an adversarial relationship among the staff functions and business units?

How committed are our people to helping each other regardless of who and where they work? Do our people check their own personal agendas at the door? What strategic uncertainties keep them awake at night? If they owned this business what would be on their horizons? Is this their Candy Store?

Out of this I can craft the next quarter, next year's strategy and vision with their help, as I now have a baseline. I will use many different types of communication methods—town hall, face to face, written and video communication—depending on the subject and the audience. In the first 100 days, I intend to be visible and a good listener and manage expectations.

I am sure this document will be added to as I learn more about this opportunity, and it is a very good start to an exciting journey. If you have additional questions, please let me know. Rebecca is working on my calendar to achieve these results in the most efficient manner possible over the next few weeks.

Thanks,

Joe

Joe put down his 100-day plan, took a deep breath, and thought, *Success will always come down to the degree to which you can get everyone in your organization at every level to understand, embrace, emulate, and execute the vision and the strategy.*

Over the years Joe may have had to change his speed and approach but not the vision, the mission, or his values. Regardless of his level or position in the organization, as a leader Joe always believed he must set the standard of what good looked like and this 100-Day Plan was a great start.

THE LESSON:
PERSPECTIVE AND VISION

» You make a great first impression when your people see that you have a vision for the business and you have a plan.

» As you work the 100-day plan look to develop strategies that capitalize on the organization's unique strengths and capabilities.

CHAPTER 16

THE BIG EIGHT

As Joe finished reading his 100-Day Plan he looked at his watch and realized most of the day had gone by filled with great pride and memories but little progress on organizing his stuff. He rationalized that organizing your office doesn't have to be done quickly or in a day. Maybe it can be done a little at a time so he could appreciate the wonderful memories.

Either way, maintaining an organized office was going to be his commitment. That was his story and he was sticking to it. Now, Adrianne buying the story was another story.

As he was diving through another box he saw an envelope marked Syracuse and with a smile opened it. He had a good idea what was in it. Snow and winter aside, Syracuse was a great assignment filled with warm and colorful people.

Syracuse is a city that sits at the corner of the Finger Lakes region in Upstate New York. Syracuse had a strong manufacturing history with significant growth after World War II. Two of the Big Three automobile manufacturers (General Motors and Chrysler) had major operations in the area. It was headquarters for Carrier Corporation, Crouse-Hinds signal manufacturing, and General Electric, which had its main television manufacturing plant at Electronics Parkway in Syracuse.

The assignment gave him the opportunity to visit great cities like Rome, Utica, Cortland, Binghamton, and the capital city and region of Albany. Upstate New York has no shortage of great scenery and places to visit. Lake George, Lake Placid, and Saratoga Raceway provide both beauty and wonderful history to explore. Halls of fame have a prominent place in Upstate New York as well, with the Baseball Hall of Fame in Cooperstown, the International Boxing Hall of Fame in Canastota, and the National Soccer Hall of Fame in Oneonta.

From a business perspective he counted it as an important learning experience with a staff of managers who were seasoned and savvy and took him under their wings.

He chuckled when he thought about his second staff meeting. It was August and the group was going through the *Farmer's Almanac* prior to the start of the meeting. He wondered what this conversation could be about. He quickly learned that in a few months the weather would be the topic of conversation and they were getting prepared. Sitting around the conference table, they were having a spirited debate similar to what he thought the Founding Fathers would have had.

Why was this such an important decision, he wondered, and why so early in the season and more importantly, what was the decision?

Their decision or bet on the weather was based on two key factors: the almanac, which they counted as their data source, and the empirical data of their guts. The dilemma: do they pay by the plow at 10 dollars per plow or do they take the seasonal rate of $300?

Joe being a bit naive about the weather and more importantly about lake-effect snow asked the question, Do you think you would get 30 snowfalls of over 3 inches (the minimum needed for an official plow) in a season? The looks he got in retrospect were priceless. They ranged from Do you know where you live? to Do you own a snow shovel or better yet a snow blower?

They proceeded to give him a history lesson on weather in his new home. Syracuse has a humid climate best known for its snowfall. Boasting 115.6 inches on average, Syracuse receives the most annual snow of any metropolitan area in the country. The city usually wins the Golden Snowball Award among upstate New York cities, and the year before he relocated there it had a record snowfall of 192.1 inches.

Without hesitation Joe became a part of the discussion. The decision: they would roll the dice and go with the per-plow quote as they rationalized it couldn't snow that much two years in a row.

Well, they were right that year: they beat the lake-effect snow with their per-plow decision and spent on average $130 for that season.

With a smile and a chuckle, it was time to get back to the envelope. He opened it and, just as he thought, he had a set of rosary beads and a prayer card from the Vatican in it. It was given to him by one of his managers, Vito, after their family trip to Rome. He kept it as one of the kindest, most thoughtful gifts he had received over his career.

The rosary beads, the prayer card, and Vito's thoughtfulness brought Joe's thoughts back to his last flight but, more importantly, Nonna. He wondered how she and her family were doing and he smiled as he thought back to some of the conversations they had had.

One of the moments that brought a smile to his face happened toward the end of the flight. Nonna had been sleeping soundly when she twitched and woke herself up. A bit startled she looked over at Joe and said, "Ciao. Quanto tempo ancora? Dov'è il bagno?" The little Italian he knew was able to interpret "Hello How much longer and do you know where the bathroom is?"

All questions he could answer. They were about 30 minutes out and the bathroom was in the back but he thought it would be okay for her to use the one in the front. She agreed as the walk to the back was too far for her. As they were unbuckling their seat belts he looked up and saw the activity in front of the flight cabin door; this could only mean that one of the pilots needed to use the rest room as well. Just then the DING went off, this time instructing the passengers to please take their seats, as the pilot was going to use the rest room.

A very specific process had to be followed as part of new security procedures. Joe explains to Nonna what is happening and with 30 minutes' left. She buckles her seat belt, looks at Joe, and says, "It wasn't meant to be," and falls back asleep.

As everything was positioned, the door opens and the crew member leaves the flight cabin and enters the restroom. Through the open door, Joe notices and marvels at all the gauges and instruments that a pilot must monitor to operate a plane's engines and controls to navigate and fly the airplane. Joe reasoned that a pilot, like a good leader, must be an effective decision maker.

What separated a good manager from a great one in Joe's view was the drive to never stop learning. Joe was very proud of his cousin, Peter, who was a doctor. Peter not only had great bedside manner but had an insatiable desire to continually learn and be the best doctor he could be. He learned from his patients and from conversations with his peers, and he could always be caught on the beach reading about his profession and gaining new insights into the world of medicine.

Joe himself always preached that there is a world outside your office. There are people in your organization at all levels you can learn from as well as customers and other professionals. Joe believed that no one was more important than anyone else, which opened the lines of communication and broke down the barriers to learning.

A leader, like a pilot or a doctor, needs to monitor the critical areas for success. Peter had his critical readings and markers for his patients and Antonio for his airplane. Joe had his dashboard of critical elements that were leading indicators he and his team monitored on a daily basis. These leading indicators would then drive the results of the lagging indicators. In Dr. Peter's world, the leading indicators would be the patients' blood pleasure, temperature, weight, etc. For Antonio, speed, altitude, and fuel consumption were some of his.

For Joe, it could be things like the number of injuries and accidents, employee turnover, the number of days to collect. All these are the leading indicators that if on plan should lead to the lagging indicators being on plan, which should lead to a successful business. Or in the case of Dr. Peter, a healthy patient.

Joe called his indicators, his dashboard, the Big Eight. The Big Eight starts and ends with people, as does growth and flawless execution.

For example, are associates adopting safety as a core value? Do they look for ways to serve the unique needs of customers with energy, creativity, and enthusiasm for the business? Do they approach each opportunity as a brand ambassador? Do they recognize opportunities to improve execution and fix internal and external issues? Regardless of the problem, the solution always started with the help of our people. Joe's Big Eight (or dashboard for success) had developed over time and may vary by business or operation. The key is to have a view of what good looks like and then monitor and adjust to stay on course.

1. SAFETY AS A CORE VALUE

Safety is an integral part of our people feeling like valued individuals. When our people see that we care enough about them and that we will not let them work in an unsafe manner they understand our commitment to them and safety. Safety is a core value and something that we will never compromise. The solutions we provide our customer will always have a safety component. Through training, communications, and personal accountability, we are committed to instilling a safety culture throughout our organization. It is our way to be "safe and thoughtful" in our approach to our business. This includes doing things safely, thoughtfully, and efficiently the first time.

2. DIVERSIFICATION OF OUR CUSTOMER BASE AND ORGANIC GROWTH

To grow our business requires a deep understanding of our service portfolio and the markets we serve. In doing so, we will market what we do well. We will sell where there is opportunity to go deeper and wider with current customers and where there is prospective business with new customers in new markets that span the enterprise. To grow organically, we must all be salespeople and brand ambassadors—always striving for opportunities to promote our business. We all serve in the role of growing our business.

3. INCREASE RETURN ON INVESTED CAPITAL

Return on invested capital (ROIC) is a financial measure that quantifies how efficiently a company allocates its cash investments relative to how much cash flow those investments generate.

Focusing on ROIC effectively allows us to show how we manage a limited pool of resources to maximize profit. When we Act Like an Owner we realize that protecting our assets to extend their useful life and leveraging investments to maximize business process improvements and cost reductions increase our ROIC. Always ask, is our investment return greater than our risk? If I was writing the check from my personal checking account, would I write the check?

4. REDUCE DEBT TO IMPROVE OPERATIONAL LEVERAGE

Operating leverage is a measure of how our revenue growth translates into growth in operating income, which is impacted by fixed and variable costs. While there are many ways to measure this, two ways each and every one of us can help make exponential gains are by (1) growing the business and (2) reducing expenses and the company's use of cash. Look at our business through the lens of Balanced Leadership and Act Like an Owner to create positive operating leverage. Doing it right the first time will always lead to a great start.

5. IMPROVE CAPITAL STRUCTURE

Our capital structure is how we finance our overall operations and growth by using different sources of funds. It is measured by a leverage ratio of total debt to EBITDA (earnings before interest, tax, depreciation, and amortization). For us running our day to day operations and having low capital expenditures plus an efficient and profitable operating strategy will equal a high level of free cash flow. Other ways we can help is by understanding customers' requirements to bill and collect quickly and properly in the shortest time possible. We can also organize resources to reduce accounts receivables and unbilled work to achieve days sales outstanding targets.

6. GENERATE FREE CASH FLOW

Free cash flow represents the cash that we are able to generate after paying for our assets and expenses such as salaries, vendors, facilities, equipment, etc. When we have a positive cash flow, we will be able to better pay down debt and invest in our business and our people to increase growth in the new market segments we've identified. By making thoughtful and deliberate decisions, we can build new opportunities to generate free cash flow and reduce our debt to secure an optimal capital structure.

7. LESS VOLATILE EARNINGS

A well-balanced business has well-balanced earnings. By defining new segments and services and selling existing solutions in new geographical markets, we can ensure consistency in our earnings throughout the year. This will create a steady stream of revenue, in addition to our traditional quarterly peak. It also gives us the best opportunity to maximize the use of our fixed assets.

8. BE THE BEST PEOPLE IN THE INDUSTRY

Being the best is something to strive for each day. It is an innate force and powerful state of mind visible to others through a determined and enthusiastic can-do attitude. We intend to be the best-educated and safest solutions provider connecting customers with leading technologies across specific market segments. We will be the best fully integrated solutions partner everyone wants to do business with. We aspire to have the best, the brightest, the most informed, and best-educated people in the industry; we want this to be an aspiration of our people as well.

At different times Joe would have conversations with various people at all levels about the significance of the elements or if they were the right elements. Joe was always consistent in his questions: What are your expectations, what are the results you are holding yourself and your people accountable to, and what are the consequences of achieving or not achieving these results?

To Joe it wasn't the number of elements or the way you packaged them. Rather they had to pass the "if then, go to" test. If Joe identified the true problems and their solution and he has achieved all the results identified in the solution, then he should be able to go to the final product and see the success. If he met all the elements but did not achieve the desired results, then he picked the wrong elements or addressed the wrong problem. It was about having the vision, knowing the goals and measures, and achieving success.

He also wanted to make sure everyone understood that reporting the numbers was only a step in the process. Although an important one, it was just that, a step. It was what you did with the information that separated "news reporters" from "news makers." Joe wanted news makers; there were plenty of news reporters.

THE LESSON:
USE SIMPLE BUT EFFECTIVE METRICS
TO TRACK BOTH ORGANIZATIONAL
EFFECTIVENESS AND EFFICIENCY.

» Demand high performance.

» Build and sustain a culture of continuous improvement.

» Define your list of critical performance metrics to monitor.

» Believe strongly in cause and effect.

» Be a news maker, not a news reporter.

CHAPTER 17
ACADEMY ADDRESS

The week went by quicker than Joe thought it would. He woke each day with a purpose and a plan to get something accomplished he had put off.

Some of the things he looked forward to in his retirement were spending time with Adrianne and with the kids. They had always talked about spending more time at their beach house on the Jersey Shore. They also spoke about doing some traveling, both domestically and internationally. They thought a fun trip would be to visit the people and places they lived in to get caught up with the many great families they had met and spent time with along the way. They also thought it would be interesting to see things from a different time and perspective.

Personally he wanted to get in some quality time with the kids and experience and share in their grown-up lives. Three of the four were married and starting their own families.

The oldest, Jean Marie, was an elementary special education teacher and a cheerleading coach. She was the recipient of the Teacher of the Year award in her school district and had great passion for her profession and coaching. Jean Marie and her husband, Kris, were also the parents of Nico, Joe, and Adrianne's first grandchild.

Number two was Nicole; she was also married. Sean and Nicole recently bought a house and were experiencing all the excitement of their new purchase. Nicole was a producer on an Emmy Award–winning daytime television program. She was a shining example of promotion from within in her career.

Number three was their first son, Rocco Anthony. He was the most recently married, to a wonderful bride named Jennifer. He began his career after graduation as a college hockey coach. As a former player both in high school and college, he followed this path and pursued his passion for the game and love of coaching.

The reality of marriage and starting a family led to a career change with a more consistent cash flow as a salesperson in a well-known Fortune 500 company. He has gotten off to a great start and, like he did on the ice, approaches everything with great energy and enthusiasm.

Maturity is sometimes knowing when to put some things on hold for a better time. Learning to prioritize is not always easy or fun but a necessary skill in life and business.

Adrianne and Joe felt blessed to have two great sons-in-law and a wonderful daughter-in-law as additions to the family.

Number four was Andrew Vincent, Mr. Greater Than and Less Than. He certainly turned out greater than! Excellence is no accident but the result of hard work and attention to details. Andrew and his siblings live this creed. He graduated college after his four years of playing college baseball and is now a baseball coach himself at the college level.

Like Nonna, Adrianne and Joe felt blessed with four great kids, all with great spouses and, in the case of Andrew, a significant other.

Joe was proud of who they had become, individuals whose success was best described not in wealth, position, or title but in values, integrity, and work ethic. Each of them could be described as characters but they each had character. They all enjoyed coaching, mentoring, and directing. As similar as they were culturally and ethically, their greatest strength lay in their individual talents and style.

Great teams, great organizations, and great families are made of great individuals who understand, embrace, emulate, and execute the vision and strategy of the organization and the team. It is no different in a family. The mission and value statements may not be hanging on walls throughout the office and locker rooms but are discussed around the kitchen table and played out day to day in the way you live your life.

Organizations, teams, and families understand that healthy discourse is disagreeing without being disagreeable. This is the environment that will Only Accept a Person's Best.

Employees, teammates, and family members often live up to the expectations of them whether the expectations are high or low, so it makes sense to keep expectations high, but realistic. If you expect them to be sloppy or uncooperative—and communicate that expectation to them—you usually will get what you expect. However, if you have high but realistic expectations of your employees, teammates, and family members, they often will work hard to meet your expectations.

Joe had many opportunities to speak in front of groups both large and small. As one of his last requests he was asked to speak at a local prep school. Joe enjoyed these opportunities to interact with the community and especially the next generation of leaders. He eagerly accepted these speaking engagements because they provided opportunities for mutual learning experiences. It was also an opportunity to teach and mentor and give back to the next generation, something he had hoped his children might have learned from him.

This particular speech was very special to him and was a labor of love to write. He used this speech as an opportunity to talk about his children, family, and career highlights. He was especially proud of his children and the models of excellence they had become. He also profiled great moments that were rewarding, educational, and profound in his career.

He was truly honored to represent the important topic of character and values. These were all topics of conversation he had with his dad as a child and ones he had with his children as a father. They were also important conversations he had with his people as a leader. Joe titled the speech "Why Values Matter." This was a belief he had great conviction in and one he felt led to defining moments for people and companies.

To this point, his filing and organizing had not uncovered the speech. He frantically looked through some of the papers he had filed and stored again to find the speech. Hmmmm, no speech. Next he looked through some folders and the last box but still no speech. He took a deep breath and thought what to do next. Does he go through all the boxes again?

He could have gone through all the files again but he took the old-fashioned Italian Catholic approach: he prayed to Saint Anthony, the patron saint you pray to when you lose something. The prayer is simple: Good Saint Anthony come around, something's lost that can't be found.

After a few minutes he thought, *I haven't looked in the last calendar*, which was still in his briefcase. Well, there it was! Thank you, Saint

Anthony. Hey, just saying.

With a sigh of relief, he took a moment to read the speech and it brought back those great memories and thoughts.

Joe had many great honors in his long career. Some honors were through achievement and some were in meeting the people and seeing the many places his career had taken him.

Joe, like his children now, had a passion for coaching. He felt great leaders were great coaches, so he never felt he compromised or gave up on his coaching passion. One of Joe's greatest thrills that he spoke about in the speech was when he was assigned to a team of leaders to prepare a talk for an upcoming management conference.

He realized the topic of the talk they were asked to prepare had many similarities to a talk he had just heard the legendary Coach John Wooden give in Anaheim, California.

Coach Wooden was a coaching icon and one of Joe's personal role models and a life teacher.

Joe took a chance and reached out to Coach Wooden through the athletic department at UCLA, where Coach Wooden and Joe got connected.

Chances are good that someday you'll meet someone famous. Maybe it is a sports figure or an actor or actress you have enjoyed, but the thrill of meeting a legendary coach whom you admired and often quoted was a dream come true. Coach Wooden was both gracious to help him with this assignment and hospitable as they met and spoke in his home. Joe counted this as one of the incredible moments in a wonderful career. After this meeting and conversation, UCLA coach John Wooden was an integral part of the world according to Joe.

Coach Wooden has been called one of the most respected coaches in the history of sports and the most successful coach in men's college basketball history. Under his leadership, the Bruins achieved many accomplishments, including a record 10 NCAA men's basketball championship titles. Many believe the records set under Coach Wooden's leadership are unbreakable.

He was also well known for his inspirational theories. At the meeting, during the interview, and in all of the future readings, Coach Wooden helped shape his professional life and values. Coach Wooden identified two cornerstones that laid the foundation for his "Pyramid of Success"—industriousness and enthusiasm.

Industriousness, as Wooden defined it, is more than just showing up and going through the motions. It is work, hard work. It is the ability to not only work hard but to continue to improve.

On the other end of the structure is enthusiasm. Enthusiasm is the heart behind the hard work. Joe learned and added his personal touch over time that "Hard work without enthusiasm is just that—hard work." Enthusiasm is the ability to reach your full potential, to prepare and perform at your highest level. It's also contagious. It brushes off on those you work with, those you work for, and the ones you lead.

It was no coincidence that with such an admiration for Coach Wooden and his philosophies that Joe's management style and approach had many similarities. Joe had one significant difference, however. Coach Wooden coached many successful players over his career and this had its challenges from both an ego and individual personality perspective.

Both Joe and Coach Wooden were fortunate to coach, teach, and mentor some excellent individuals who went onto very successful careers, Coach Wooden in the basketball arena and Joe in the business arena.

In Joe's view the significant difference was the honesty of purpose in the people he managed, worked with, and mentored. It pertains to your motivation, to the pursuit of your goals and dreams. No name in lights or sneaker contracts for the working person. The reality is you're going to have to work at whatever it is you hope to achieve in your life. But it's how you face it and the journey you take that speaks to your character.

Your true character is defined by your honesty of purpose. Your purpose is sacred and authentic. Honesty is what's at the core of your moral character. It's being trustworthy, loyal, fair, sincere, and true, even when it is difficult to be. It is not only how you create your values, but also how you add value to the lives of others.

Academic excellence, character development, personal motivation, physical development and leadership all require you to perform at your best—with honesty of purpose. You cannot develop your character or motivate yourself or lead others unless you have truly defined your purpose—your intent.

This does not necessarily mean you must know your calling in life or exactly what you want to be when you leave school, but you do need to be clear about and strongly aware of your values, goals, and character.

Joe was blessed to land his first job with a great company with a rich heritage and culture. It was a company that provided a lifetime of career opportunities through its "promotion from within" culture. Today, it's unusual to remain with a company for an entire career.

These principles, values, and culture are still as valuable today as they were over 100 years ago. The company's purpose was clear, simple, and honest.

What is truly unique about companies like this is the values and work ethic instilled in its people across the world. It creates a sense of camaraderie that you will always have with the organization and the people you work with in the organization. You become a work family.

So what do some of the world's greatest companies have in common? They began as small businesses, usually with an entrepreneur with a dream or a vision. Service was usually their calling card. Many times they started in small towns and cities like Seattle or Bellevue, Washington; Cupertino, California; Milwaukee, Wisconsin; Moline, Illinois; or Schenectady, New York. These companies did well despite stiff competition or as new entries into their markets, largely because of their strict policies of customer courtesy, reliability, round-the-clock service, and a desire to succeed.

This honesty of purpose became a point of differentiation for many companies and it can make the difference for you as you enter the job market and take on new assignments and responsibilities.

It was the company's early culture of honesty and trustworthiness—including the proper appearance of its people and company assets, along with their courtesy, that gave it a competitive edge. You want to be seen as a person as comfortable on the shop floor as you are in the front offices. Your honesty of purpose can grant you front-door access but your hard work and ethical behavior will keep you there. It's something that many might take for granted today, but it will define you as a person and a leader. Someday you would like to be defined as the gold standard of service and professionalism.

For Joe, this culture was instilled with him from his dad and family and reinforced at a great company. He did not know what to expect on his first day, but he knew they were going to get the best of his abilities. He met some interesting people in those first few days. Some even told him to work slower: no one really knew how good or bad a job you really did. As they walked away, Joe said to himself, one person does, ME. Once again he heard his dad: it is what you do when no is watching that counts. It seemed to be overwhelming at times as he was working his way through college. Joe was always working to improve himself and work to the highest level of his ability but frankly it was not easy.

Young companies and young people expand their knowledge base and grow into world-class companies and people. No person or company starts at the top. Some of the great American companies are stronger today because of their ability to evolve and persevere with the same honesty of purpose infused into its culture at its inception.

We are known for our values and the things we aspire to be and ultimately what we achieve as people and companies. It all starts with your values and then what you do when no one is watching that defines who you are, what you stand for, and what you won't compromise as a person and a business.

It shaped Joe's character and it's what he hoped to pass along to others in his charge.

Whether we realize it or not, we are all here to determine what our real intent is in life. Purpose-driven people put their morals, character, and honesty first. Without purpose, we drift. With purpose, we steer.

You have the responsibility to yourself and to others to use your best judgment, weigh your options carefully, and make the right decisions—even if they're not the most favorable or popular—even when no one is watching!

When you do that, you honor yourself and your values. Wherever your path takes you, know that your trustworthiness is your highest honor. For if you are a trusted leader, others will believe in your vision, mission, and values and will trust in you enough to follow you, whether in business or in life.

Joe thought how lucky he was to have these opportunities to address groups like this. These were the moments that Joe felt like you can leave someplace a better place than you found it. It was his way of saying thank you to all those people who had touched him along the way.

He thought it is good to be constructively dissatisfied and strive for continuous improvement. But maybe the nun that taught him in fifth grade said it best: "You may be disappointed where you are in relationship to others, but where you are from where you started may be a more rewarding story and a better evaluation."

Joe never pictured himself giving a speech or leading groups of people as he sat in that fifth-grade classroom. In fact, he did not enjoy public speaking or the attention that came with it. During the try-out for the fifth-grade Christmas play, Joe tried out for the part of the shepherd because there were no speaking requirements and your role was to point at the star over the manger. It's amazing how things have changed.

That was great advice and a wonderful perspective she had left with him.

THE LESSON:
CREATE AND ADD VALUE ALL ALONG
YOUR JOURNEY.

» Embracing values early in life will serve you in ways too numerous to count over a lifetime.

» Develop many touch points along the way with your people, customers, and the community.

» Establish constructive and solid interpersonal skills and relationships.

» Clearly articulate your values.

» Create an authentic culture to ensure an open, candid, trusting relationship that you are proud to share.

CHAPTER 18
YOUR LEGACY

Some time had passed and Joe was working hard on his new career retirement when he got a call from an old friend and business partner named Tim. Joe had great respect for Tim as a person and a business professional. Joe had told Adrianne that his best retirement gift was the news that Tim received the promotion he so rightfully deserved. Tim was given an excellent assignment, but one that had its share of difficulties and complexities. Joe had complete confidence in Tim and had no doubt he was the right person for the job. Joe was excited to hear his voice and was anxious to get caught up with him.

Joe quickly asked Tim, "How are you? How are things going?"

Tim replied, "Joe, before we get caught up on my side, how are you and Adrianne doing in retirement?" Joe explained he was banned from food shopping; it seems that adding to the grocery list is not viewed as adding value or going to where the puck is going. In this new world it means, "You think I forgot something or I did not put together a complete list! I am working on my new approach. She likes the lug nut story and does reference it, which makes me very happy; however, if you overuse it, you quickly move to lug head status."

Joe was getting caught up on all the doctors' appointments he missed during his working days. The doctor's office he told Tim is where you meet some of the most interesting people and it can put things into perspective quickly. The other day he met a 103-year-old woman. She was upbeat and personable and was interested in knowing about his family and what he was doing since his retirement. He gave her a brief update and then asked her, "What do you think is the best thing about being 103?"

She replied with a great smile, "No peer pressure."

"So, Tim, in life as in business it is all about your outlook. This wonderful, full-of-life 103-year-old woman proceeded to ask me about my health now that I am getting caught up on all the doctors' appointments." Joe told her that he had one small scare that turned out to be nothing. "What was it?" she asked. After his physical, he was told he has a cholesterol problem and he would be on this medication for the rest of his life.

She replied, "That is normal—what was the scare?"

He told her that when he received the medication, he wondered if it was more serious than they told him because the prescription bottle was marked no refills. She wisely smiled and said, "Welcome to the world of generic mail-order prescription drugs."

"So, Tim," Joe said, "I continue to learn, meet some great people, and thankfully all is good."

Joe then asked the question he really wondered about: "So how are you, my friend?"

Tim said, "I'm honored by my promotion and excited about the chance to create my legacy. It is an operation that has its challenges, but it also has its strengths and opportunities.

"Not a day goes by that I do not think about our time together. We have had the opportunity to have many different assignments. Some were in well-run operations that we needed to get to world class. These presented one set of challenges. We had a few that we had to manage through some changing times. The most challenging were those that had lost their way. Good people who felt disenfranchised, or not valued, customer churn that was high, and a business plan that was unachievable after the first quarter.

"Although these were the most challenging they were also the most rewarding. We had a plan and a vision and we were able to communicate it. Our people embraced the vision and we were able to celebrate some excellent successes.

"Joe, this is the situation I find myself in today," he continued. "I have all the energy and enthusiasm, I am committed to do the work, but frankly I do not know where to start. I have lived the Balanced Leadership approach. I understand we have a lot of loose lug nuts that need to be tightened before these important items become urgent. I have a management team that I believe has the desire to succeed but does not have the vision and path to get there. I have a meeting in a few weeks where I will have the entire team in one place at one time for a call to action."

Joe interrupted him as he sensed the frustration in his voice. "Tim, you are more than capable, prepared, and the right person for this opportunity. More importantly, you know who you are, what you stand for, and what you won't compromise! I know you put together your 100-Day Plan and are more than halfway into it. This will provide great insight into the vision and direction of your meeting and how you will rebuild your operation into a world-class group of talented professionals committed to Balanced Leadership. Tim, please don't get discouraged. Let's take a moment to take a step back and talk about you and your situation.

"Tim, we always joked, when we looked at big problems to solve, that you eat an elephant one bite at a time so you don't get overwhelmed. Your promotion is well-deserved and I know that you have accepted your leadership role and all that comes with it. It is important to set clear boundaries for all to follow and avoid any confusion. So grab your fork and let's eat this problem one bite at a time.

"You are a very good communicator but now you will have to become an effective communicator with everyone you lead. Clarity will be essential and is the most critical component of effective communication. Your people cannot do what's required unless they understand exactly what the task is, as well as your expectations of them.

"You will want to use specific terms and language that says what you mean. The people in your care should not have to guess at what you want. For example, saying 'I need this report by Friday at noon' is more specific than 'I need this report as soon as you can get to it.'

"You will also want to be direct. Get to the main point or purpose of your conversation at the beginning. When conversations begin with side issues, you often never reach the real reason for the conversation. Also, keep it simple. Simple often leads to effective communication and results. Provide your people with only the information they really need from you. Your strength has always been your down-to-earth style and approach. In this new position avoid trying to impress them with your command of the language, your knowledge of the problems, or overloading them with detail they don't need or want. Be yourself. Yourself is good—it is what got you here!

"Finally, speed and successes create momentum; they create the tipping point. To get traction avoid conflicting messages, make sure everyone gets a consistent message from you. For example, if a deadline is important, don't weaken the message by giving it in a casual, offhand manner. If you want to express your appreciation for good work and encourage the employee to continue it, save any correction or criticisms for another time. Applaud the behavior you want everyone to exhibit. This is how they will know what good looks like! Whenever two different types of messages are mixed, the effect of each is weakened.

"Now that you are the leader, the role model, this new reality must be reflected in your attitude, presence, and most importantly, through your behavior. Live by the mantra 'You cannot build a reputation on what you intend to do.' Although you will have to be action oriented, never lose sight that you get your results through others."

"Joe," Tim replied, "I cannot tell you how much I have missed these conversations, or as you often called them, talks around the kitchen table. One of your consistent themes has always been to be true to yourself and be yourself. You have always told us that the principles, values, and approach may be consistent, but the style has to be uniquely you. People are following you, not a book or a speech," Tim said. "I completely understand and want to create my style to support and drive the principles of Balanced Leadership. I will need to be an efficient and effective communicator as I describe to my team: who we are, what we stand for, and what we won't compromise as a group.

"My request is my best way to say thank you for your guidance and leadership. I think you will understand and enjoy it. The last call-to-action talk you gave was an excellent summary and a synopsis of a wonderful career. I would like to use your talk as the foundation of my talk."

There was a pause on the phone after Tim finished his sentence and request.

Joe took a deep breath and told Tim he was honored and touched by his request. He could feel free to use as much or as little as he would like or need.

"The fact that you would like to incorporate some of my thoughts into your vision is what legacy is all about," he said. "Thank you for the honor, but remember it has to be you. You set the tone from the top, you set the pace, and you live the values."

Joe ended the call, telling Tim he made his day and made a commitment to send the speech to Tim.

Going through his files on the computer Joe found the "Call to Action Speech" and with an encouraging note attached, pushed the send button on his computer.

An emotional Joe looked up into the sky and said, "Dad, your greatest gift was that the world, our family, and I are better because of your time with us. I hope the same can be said about me, that the places I have been are a little better after I have left them."

It was at that moment that Joe understood what legacy was all about. Legacy was the greatest gift he received and the greatest gift you can give to others.

Although his dad never officially coached a sports team, he had all the qualities of a great teacher, coach, and mentor.

I think Coach Wooden had the best description of character and reputation. Joe believed if Coach Wooden had met his dad he would agree that his description fit his dad. Coach Wooden said, "Ability may get you to the top, but it takes character to keep you there." And "Be more concerned with your character than your reputation. Your character is what you really are, while your reputation is merely what others think you are."

Your character is your legacy; it is what you leave behind. It can be seen in the people and places you have touched.

Joe's dad probably did not know what his calling in life would be when he left Italy as a young boy looking for a new life in the United States or exactly what he wanted to be when he got here, but he was clear about and strongly aware of his values, goals, and ethics, which became his character and the legacy he left behind.

As Joe was growing up, he never really thought in terms of honor codes and cornerstones. He just knew there were certain things he needed to focus on, to do, and to achieve. Coach Wooden was, and has been, an outstanding role model and business mentor in Joe's adult life.

A very simple and unassuming man with great integrity and character, his dad, said it best to Joe and his two brothers and sister as they were growing up. It is the life lesson and standard that he judged himself by and strove to instill in all those he came in contact with.

He said to him one day, "It's what you do when no one is watching that counts!" As a young man who sometimes got off track, Joe would say, "Dad, that is the best part—no one is watching."

As he grew, took on more responsibility, and became hopefully a mentor and role model for others, he came to understand that leadership, integrity, and honesty of purpose is what you do when no one is watching! It's a simple message from a simple man, with a very powerful meaning!

As you grow and develop, take on new challenges or simply move into a new phase of your life, you will be faced with complications and adversity that may set you back. Honesty, perseverance, and trustworthiness will become major factors in overcoming these obstacles and creating your personal brand and your legacy.

Along the way you come to a decision point or stage gate. Your choice is simple but profound in each instance but a decision must be made. Your choices are

LEAD, FOLLOW, or GET OUT OF THE WAY

If you choose to lead you will need to be an honest and trusted leader in order to establish your vision, mission, and values so that those in your care or supervision will trust you enough to follow.

As a lifelong learner, you are constantly forging a path to transform yourself into a high-character, high-performance leader. You will never be without challenges both in life and business. But if you are focused and ready to face these complex business challenges and personal changes with discipline, determination, honesty of purpose, and in an ethical manner you will be successful.

Whether we realize it or not, we are all here to determine what our real intent is in life. For each of us it may be different. For Joe, it was being a great spouse, father, leader, and mentor; to have a legacy, to leave the place a little better than he found it.

Purpose-driven people put their morals, character, and honesty first.

Without purpose, we drift. With purpose, we steer.

You have a responsibility to yourself and to others to use your best judgment, weigh your options carefully, and make the right decisions—even if they're not the most favorable or popular, even when no one is watching!

When you do that you honor yourself and your values. Wherever your path takes you, know that your trustworthiness is your highest honor. For if you are a trusted leader, others will believe in your vision, mission, and values and will trust in you enough to follow you. That will be your legacy.

As a person your core beliefs are not what you would like them to be, but rather what actually lives and breathes in you as a person. The good news is that you will have many opportunities in a career and in life to demonstrate these values and beliefs, but only one chance to get it right each time.

Live your word. Leave a Legacy.

THE LESSON:

CREATE YOUR LEGACY. CONTINUOUS
IMPROVEMENT AND DEVELOPMENT REQUIRES
CONSTANT CALIBRATION AND OPTIMIZES
PERFORMANCE.

» Instill continuous learning as a foundation of business success.

» Pass along your legacy as a Balanced Leader. The people in your care as well as your customers and stakeholders will thank you with their loyalty, the most sustainable dividend.

» Leave it a little better than you found it.

ROCKY ROMANELLA is the Founder and CEO of 3SIXTY Management Services, LLC, a management consulting firm specializing in Executive Speaking, Leadership Development, and Consulting Services. Rocky is an experienced leader who led one of the largest rebranding initiatives in franchising history – The UPS Store, revolutionizing the $9 billion retail shipping and business services market. Through his executive roles and leadership advisory services, Rocky delivers results by developing and implementing his Balanced Leadership Model across enterprise operations, including a laser focus on customer needs, employee empowerment, and the demands of shareholders and stakeholders.

Rocky possesses a clear vision of the changing business landscape, the passion to develop strategies, and the tactics and metrics to drive results. He lives in New Jersey with his wife. This is his first book.